40+ Ways to Increase Organizational Clarity, Alignment and Performance

James O'Gara

Contents

CHAPTER 1
Achieving Organizational Clarity and Alignment

CHAPTER 2
Regain Control of Your Corporate Story and Strategy

CHAPTER 3
Strategic Communication: Before, During &
After M&A

CHAPTER 4
How CEO Messaging and Communication Impacts Business Results

CHAPTER 5
Voice of the CEO and C-Suite: A Defining Factor in Organizational Performance

CHAPTER 6
Clarity (or Lack Thereof) and Its Direct Impact on Business Performance

CHAPTER 10
Employee Buy-in and Customer Buying Requirements Have Changed. Has Your Business?

CHAPTER 11
Leveraging Real Customer Insights and Stories to Accelerate Growth

Introduction

For the past 18 years as the founder and CEO of OnMessage, I have been fortunate to work with C-suite executives at literally hundreds of high-growth and Fortune 1000 companies. Much of the work I have done has been helping these leaders leverage the power and influence of communications to achieve desired business results. More specifically, leveraging internal and external messaging, positioning and communication strategies to increase organizational clarity, alignment and performance.

This book is a compilation of knowledge gained and lessons learned from thousands of hours working side by side, in the trenches with business leaders across a wide range of industries. Each chapter focuses on a specific macro-topic or challenge. Then, within each chapter, you will find four to five stories and recommendations to help you improve performance in this area through effective communications strategies.

This is not a novel or biography. Rather a collection of independent stories and insights <u>designed to be read and pondered individually</u>. In total, there are more than 40+ techniques and recommendations included within the book.

You can start your journey anywhere you would like. Pick a chapter or topic that speaks to you, then read one or all of the stories within that section. Jump from one story and chapter to the next. Your goal is to find nuggets of knowledge and inspiration that will help you improve performance in specific areas of your business. You will find a few intentional themes repeated throughout the book. These themes contain the secret to leveraging communication as a strategic advantage in the marketplace.

Ultimately, my intention in compiling this collection of lessons learned and strategic recommendations was to get C-suite and business leaders, like yourself, to think differently about how you communicate internally and externally. To help you understand the power and influence that communication can have on business results. While every chapter and story may not pertain to specific challenges that your company faces right here, right now — I am confident you will uncover a number of actionable insights that you can use to increase clarity, alignment and performance across your organization.

CHAPTER I

Achieving Organizational Clarity and Alignment

Lack of Clarity in Your Corporate Story and Strategy Is Costing You

As a C-suite executive or leader, you know there is nothing more important than clarity. Clarity in the story you want to tell. Clarity in the strategy you want to execute.

When a company is just starting out, the company's story and strategy are crystal-clear to everyone. But then two things happen.

1. Growth.
2. Change.

As a company grows — the organization becomes more complex with more employees, organizational silos, products, customers, partners, etc.

As time passes — changes take place in the business, markets, competitive environment, customer requirements, etc.

Growth and change negatively impact clarity. And that is a problem, because clarity is the cornerstone of every high-performing organization. Without a clear understanding of your company's story and strategy — your organization will not perform at the highest level.

Below is an excerpt from "The Clarity Principle." It highlights a real, passionate conversation that took place among C-suite executives and illustrates how growth and change negatively impact organizational performance:

"The lack of clarity is exhausting. We, the group in the room, are not clear on the positioning. How do we expect the rest of the company to be? … If we don't pull together and operate from a common strategic framework, we are done. … Our company needs a new, simple narrative."

Has your company experienced growth? Change? Do your leaders understand the corporate story you want to tell and the strategy you need them to execute in the marketplace? What about your employees?

If you are like many other executives, growth and change have created confusion inside and outside of your company. And this lack of clarity is costing you.

Will this be the year that you and your executive team make organizational alignment a priority? The year you align leaders and employees around a unified corporate story and strategy? It should be.

Regain clarity this year. Your leadership team, employees, partners and customers will greatly appreciate it … and your business will perform at a higher level as a result.

Organizational Alignment Doesn't Happen by Chance

At times, C-suite executives and business leaders lose sight of this simple fact...

We live in a noisy, complex world.

While executives may spend hours thinking about the company's strategy and story — customers, employees and partners do not.

In fact, many business leaders are amazed to learn that 70 percent of all employees are unknowingly misaligned with their company's strategic direction and just 55 percent of middle managers can even name one of their company's top five priorities (*Harvard Business Review*).

These executives are even more shocked when they hear that...

90 percent of their frontline employees don't know what their company stands for and what makes it different from the competition (Gallup).

In the chaotic business world we operate in today, organizational clarity and alignment don't happen by chance.

Executive teams that run high-performing organizations realize this. They acknowledge the critical role clarity and alignment play in business performance. They understand that for the company's strategy and story to drive optimal business performance, it must be institutionalized. To make this happen, smart C-suite executives are realigning their entire organization around a clearly defined and documented corporate strategy and story. And most importantly, they are infusing that strategy and story into the fabric of their organization and customer experience.

Is your organization lacking clarity and alignment? Well, just answer these questions:

> Has your vision evolved since the early years of the business?
> Has your organizational structure changed dramatically?
> Is your business model more complex?
> Have you launched several new products or services in recent years?
> Do you have new leaders and managers in place across the company?
> Has your sales organization grown in size or experienced turnover?
> Have you recently completed a merger or acquisition?
> Has your leadership team grown or changed dramatically?
> Are more than 30 percent of your employees new to the company in the last 3–5 years?
> Are you losing top talent because they lack connectivity to your company's purpose?

If you answered yes to even one of these questions, there is a good chance that "lack of clarity and alignment" exists within your organization.

Growth, change and time create confusion. And this is costing you in more ways than you can imagine. Misaligned leaders. Wasted organizational energy. Disengaged employees. Confused customers. And so much more.

Perhaps the article, "When CEOs Talk Strategy, Is Anyone Listening?" in *Harvard Business Review* said it best...

"Just imagine, if the vision is unclear, 70% of your company doesn't know what they are striving toward and operating on false assumptions, your team will move slowly and defensively rather than swiftly and proactively. Worst of all, they might be off and running, applying valuable energy in the wrong direction."

A clear and comprehensive understanding of the company's strategy and story aligns the organization, increasing business performance. It serves as the connective tissue that holds the organization together and keeps it performing at optimal levels.

Is lack of clarity and alignment negatively impacting your business? Is it causing leaders, employees and partners to underperform?

If so, it's time to fix it.

Make this the year you regain organizational clarity and alignment ... and reach your business's true potential.

Is Your Company Going Through an Identity Crisis?

Every leadership team and company goes through it. The company grows. The vision becomes blurry, the strategy becomes less obvious across the organization. The company loses sight of its core purpose.

It happens. The question is, as a C-suite executive, what do you do about it?

Most companies think a new corporate slogan, branding campaign or company meeting will do the trick. Others simply choose to ignore it and convince themselves it isn't negatively impacting business performance. Nothing could be further from the truth.

Clarity is the key to achieving optimal performance.

Just look at the top sports teams. Look at the market leaders across different industries. They perform at the highest level because everyone in the organization — from the boardroom to the frontline — has clarity. Clarity about who they are, where they are going and how they create value.

However, as sports teams and businesses change, clarity can fade.

> Leadership changes.
> The players come and go.
> The game plan evolves.
> What it takes to win changes.

As business owners and executives, we all know that you can't stop time and you can't avoid change. However, when time passes and things change — you must re-center the business. You must regain clarity in your identity as an organization.

Some say we are in a constant state of change so what's the point? To some degree this is true. However, who you are, why you exist and the core value you deliver to customers — should not be in constant flux. In fact, these are the cornerstones of your strategy (vision, mission and values) and the essence of your corporate story (promise, value proposition, positioning, etc.). They should anchor the entire organization. They should center customer communication and engagement. They should drive employee engagement, not cause confusion. Your strategy and story should guide decisions and actions by leaders and employees across the organization.

Has your organization gone through change? Does your organization have an identity crisis?

Will this be the year you invest the time and energy to clearly redefine your company's purpose, who you are, what you do and the value you deliver? And not just in the minds of a select few executives — but up and down your entire organization? Is this the year you will use organizational alignment and clarity as a strategic advantage to drive growth in the marketplace?

Ultimately, you have two choices. Ignore the lack of clarity that exists in your organization and the negative impact it is having on business performance, or do something about it.

As a C-suite executive...the choice is yours.

The Connective Tissue That Produces High-Performing Companies

Many executives think purpose is paramount to business success. Others believe a rock-solid, go-to-market strategy is what defines market leaders. Some see the company's core values as the cornerstone of organizational success. And still other executives believe telling a differentiated, customer-centered corporate story is what drives business performance.

The truth is, each executive is right ... and they are all wrong.

Individually, these four dimensions of your business will only lift organizational performance so much, for so long. However, when all four are fully aligned and activated, companies can achieve sustained growth and positive business results.

1. Purpose (North Star)
Your reason for being, the mark your company wants to leave in the universe.

2. Go-to-Market Strategy
Your vision and mission as well as annual enterprise strategic initiatives.

3. Core Values
Shared mindset, behaviors and actions across the business.

4. Corporate Story
Your company's positioning, value proposition and promise to customers.

All four of these dimensions are critical to achieving clarity throughout your organization. All four must be aligned to drive sustained business results. Collectively, they represent the connective tissue that creates high-performing, market-leading companies.

While most executives have spent some time documenting and defining each of these elements, very few have done the work that is required to strategically align and activate these dimensions across the entire organization.

Even fewer executives have done what it takes to weave these dimensions into the fabric of their business. Why is this so critical to business success? Without organizational clarity and alignment across all four dimensions, things like this occur on a regular basis:

> Executives say one thing in external messaging and another through internal communications.
> Leaders launch initiatives that are in conflict with or have no connectivity to the company's purpose, vision or mission.
> Managers and frontline employees make decisions that do not align with the company's core values.
> Everyone seems to be overworked and busy but their collective efforts never produce the desired business results.

As a C-suite executive, you can't expect consistent words and actions to take root up and down the organization if your Purpose, Go-to-Market Strategy, Core Values and Corporate Story are not clearly defined and aligned. When these critical dimensions are not connected and clearly communicated — there is nothing with which leaders, managers and employees can align. There is no connective tissue that will drive cohesive organizational performance — from team to team, department to department or division to division.

It's just a fact: Lack of alignment and clarity negatively impact sales, customer retention, employee engagement and business performance.

Executives who are humble enough to admit this and brave enough to do something about it — will achieve success. Those who don't will continue in search of other organizational levers to pull in hopes of finding one that produces sustainable, material business results. To that group, we say ... "let us know when you find them."

CHAPTER 2

Regain Control of Your Corporate Story and Strategy

Many CEOs and Founders Have Lost It

Maybe you're the original founder of the business, maybe you are not. Regardless, when you first took the reins at your company you ...

> Were laser-focused on a clearly defined opportunity
> Developed a strategy that was simple and easy for every employee to understand
> Ensured everyone on the team was aligned with your vision and mission
> Reminded the team every day of the company's higher purpose
> Made sure everyone was clear on how the company should be positioned in the market
> You even made sure the corporate story you were sharing with customers was clear, compelling and consistent across all critical touchpoints.

Remember?

Clarity and alignment were at an all-time high. And, most likely, so was your revenue growth, customer loyalty, employee engagement and competitive differentiation in the market.

What happened? Where did that go?

"Most successful businesses start off with a clear insurgent mission on behalf of underserved customers. They are at war with their industry and each employee understands the company's bold vision — and is inspired by it. Yet as a company grows over time, this insurgent mission and sense of purpose can become diluted."

– Founder's Mentality

Every CEO knows what this quote is talking about.

There are points and times where clarity and alignment in the business is absolute. However, left unattended, clarity and alignment fades. Time passes. Organizational changes take root. The corporate strategy evolves.

The good news is, you can regain that clarity and alignment. But it requires commitment from you, your leaders and middle management. It requires an intentional plan — concerted effort and energy — up and down the organization.

Are you struggling to get your company to the next level? Has growth stalled? Is employee engagement low?

It may be for one or several of the following reasons...

> Your business strategy has gotten cloudy and employees no longer understand how they connect with the bigger picture.

> Your purpose, vision, mission and values are no longer actively embraced up and down the organization.

> Words and actions from your leadership team no longer align with or support your corporate story and strategy.

> Employees lack connection with, understanding of or belief in your corporate story and strategy.

> Customer acquisition rates are stagnant or declining because you lack a differentiated corporate story that is delivered consistently throughout the customer experience.

Maybe these are the reasons. Maybe they're not.

But the fact is, when growth stalls, when culture negatively impacts business performance and when leaders are no longer aligned — lack of clarity in your corporate story and strategy is very likely the root cause.

Recapture clarity.
The clarity you and your workforce had in your very first days.

Regain alignment.
The organizational alignment you used to drive connected decisions and actions across the business.

Companies that succeed in maintaining complete clarity and alignment between their corporate story and strategy win. They win because their words and actions are consistent; creating a superior experience that increases customer acquisition, retention, loyalty and competitive differentiation.

What Is Really Driving Your Story in the Market?

High-growth companies experience significant change. They move at a rapid pace. That's why the C-suite must be extremely diligent about maintaining organizational alignment.

Changes in fast-moving companies often originate in the R&D side of the house. Changes in solution and service offerings based on customer requirements or competitive movement. Many times, these changes impact the company's overall strategy and story.

However, very few executives stop long enough to reconnect the dots. To realign the company's go-to-market strategy (vision, mission, strategic initiatives), the company's story (positioning, value proposition, key points of difference), with the changes taking place in the company's offerings (products, solutions, services).

When this happens, the solution / service story can overtake or derail the position the company must own in the minds of its customers to experience long-term success. Ultimately, the company's vision, combined with an intimate understanding of customer requirements, should drive your product roadmap. However, when corporate and product stories get out of alignment, it creates a great deal of confusion in the minds of customers and employees. Maybe this quote from a leading product management firm says it best...

"If the executive team has not constructed, communicated or deployed the broader company strategy, the product team will have nothing to tether their product development activities to. Product and development managers who lack knowledge of the corporate strategy have no grounding from which to effectively develop useful multi-year product and technology strategies, nor tools to motivate their teams."

That's why companies must evaluate and reconnect the dots between their corporate strategy, story and their product roadmap. They must ensure that changes in the makeup of their offerings continue to align with the company's vision, mission and positioning in the market.

This won't happen if C-suite executives do not go through a formal audit and alignment process on a consistent basis. We recommend this happen at least once a year or as significant changes in the company's solutions / service offerings take place.

What's driving your story in the market?

New features and functionality? Or a larger promise to your customers? Do they align? Clarity in the minds of your customers can only exist if you tell a clear, cohesive and connected story. A corporate story that aligns with your business strategy and product roadmap.

7 out of 10 Employees Don't Know Where You / They Are Going

Did you know research shows less than 30 percent of employees know where their company is going (vision) and how they are supposed to get there (strategy)?

Ask most C-suite executives if their company's vision and strategy matter and they will say, "Of course it matters." But the real answer is uncovered when you ask the next question:

> "What are you doing to ensure clarity and alignment in your vision and strategy — up and down the organization — on a consistent basis?"

In most cases, their answer is vague and delivered with less conviction. So, let's be clear, having a vision is one thing; actually infusing that vision into the fabric of your culture is another. Defining your go-to-market strategy is one thing, translating that strategy into a message employees can understand and act on is something else.

The truth is, activating your vision and strategy is hard.

What C-suite executives must understand is that achieving organizational clarity and alignment in these areas is not a "one and done" effort. It requires intentionality at every layer of the organization. Not just within the executive team — but with every leader in the company with P&L responsibilities and direct reports.

Most executives believe they have done enough in this critical area of their business. However, industry research says otherwise. According to a *Harvard Business Review* article, "When CEOs Talk Strategy, Is Anyone Listening?" only a small percentage of employees know where their company is going (vision) and how they are going to get there (strategy).

The article includes research that shows only **29 percent of employees can correctly identify their company's strategy out of six choices.** This means 7 out of 10 employees are unknowingly misaligned with your company's vision and strategic direction.

Today, more than ever, if you want to achieve organizational alignment that will produce optimal business performance — you have to make clarity in your vision and strategy a priority.

And make no mistake, **it does matter.** According to McKinsey and Company …

"When people understand and are excited about the direction their company is taking, the company's earnings margin is twice as likely to be above the median."

Who is responsible for aligning your vision, strategy and story up and down the organization?

Who wakes up every day asking this critical question ... "What are we currently doing to ensure every employee knows where we are going and what they should be doing to help us get there?"

The Rapid Pace of Change is Changing the CEO's Role

As a CEO or C-suite executive, you are experiencing changes across your business like no generation of business leaders before. And this rapid pace of change is redefining the role of a CEO.

Specifically, in the area of strategic communications.

In the past, communication was important, but maybe not at the top of every CEO's priority list. Today, **leading executives understand the correlation between the desired outcome of change and the clarity of strategic communication around that change.**

That's why more and more CEOs are taking ownership in formulating and managing the story around strategic changes they are implementing in their business.

They are making this a high priority because they know what happens when they don't. Priorities get mixed up. Leadership decisions are not aligned. Employees get confused. Productivity drops off. And ultimately, customers get frustrated and leave.

According to Knoll Workplace Research, substantial organizational change occurs every three years.

How much has your business changed the last three months, let alone the last three years ...

> Changes in **leadership**

> Changes in **product or service offerings**

> Changes in your **selling organization**

> Changes in your **employee population**

> Changes in **customer requirements**

> Changes in your **vision and mission**

> Changes in your **operating model and business strategy**

The questions you must ask yourself are:

> Where does strategic and intentional communication land on your priority list?

> What are you doing to formulate a clear, compelling and consistent message around changes in your business and how those changes will impact leaders, frontline employees and customers?

> What story and intentional communication strategy will ensure change and innovation works for the business — not against it?

As the CEO, if you are not thinking about and leading the conversation in these areas — you should be.

Why? Because you ultimately own the impact these changes have on your business and you will not achieve desired results without an intentional, CEO-driven communication strategy that is activated up and down your organization.

CHAPTER 3

Strategic Communication: Before, During and After M&A

M&A Integration: A (Communication) Journey, Not a Destination

Anyone who has been part of an M&A transaction understands the critical nature dates and specific events play in the process. There's the letter of intent, the deal close date, public announcement and of course Day One — the day these separate companies begin the journey of becoming a single, high-performing operating entity.

All these dates are critical. However, C-suite executives need to be reminded that Day One is not the finish line. It's just the starting line. Day One is the first of many days the executive team must manage effectively to maximize the return on their M&A investment.

With that said, it's easy for the C-suite to get tunnel vision around dates and events leading up to Day One and lose sight of intentional and disciplined communication required to fully integrate two newly combined companies.

Executives often are consumed with closing the deal and then quickly hand off the rest of the journey to leaders across the organization. As a C-suite executive, what you must remember is that those leaders who are taking the handoff had day jobs before the transaction was announced. They were focused on running the existing business. The transaction brings a whole new set of integration communication responsibilities that someone (more likely a team) must own.

M&A integration communication begins the day a letter of intent is signed and continues for 12-18 months post-Day One.

> Who owns the integration messaging strategy that will guide the story inside and outside the organization?
> Who owns the communications plan?
> What about week-to-week execution of internal and external communication programs?

Successful integration communication strategies require a full-court press on these and other fronts. Not the haphazard, "we will get to it later or when we have the time," effort and attention many companies unknowingly apply in these areas.

Most executive teams fail to reap maximum value from a merger or acquisition because they short the integration communication process.

They make too many assumptions that stakeholders understand how this is supposed to work and what is expected of them. They underestimate the communication that is required to bring two cultures together. They underinvest in the disciplined and intentional communication that employees, partners and customers demand throughout the journey.

Executives who have been part of M&A transactions without a clear messaging and communications strategy have learned this the hard way.

They have experienced firsthand the chaos and confusion that takes root when a disciplined communication strategy is not executed up and down the organization.

To avoid these negative consequences, the C-suite must elevate the critical importance of communication. They must play an active role in shaping the story that will be pulled through the organization and customer experience post-announcement. These executives recognize that while HR, communications, marketing and other leaders have a role to play, a dedicated, experienced M&A integration communication team (with the expertise, processes and tools to fully integrate the companies over a defined period of time) is absolutely required for success. They value experts who have been through dozens of M&A transactions and bring the structure, strategy and tools required to drive effective integration communication inside and outside of the organization.

Are you currently planning a merger or acquisition?

Get in front of the communication requirements. Create a sustained plan of attack.

Are you experiencing chaos and confusion post-transaction?

It's not too late. Formulate a clear, consistent integration story. Build and start executing a disciplined communication plan.

In the end, it doesn't matter when you recognize the critical role integration communication plays in M&A success. It's just vital that you do. And then ... do something about it.

What's Your M&A Integration Story (Internally and Externally)?

As a C-suite executive, you know that nothing is more important during times of change than consistent communication and staying on message.

Why? Because when change occurs, humans seek clarity.

However, when your audience hears an inconsistent story, doubt and confusion creep into their minds. Doubt and confusion cripple organizational performance. This is especially true when it comes to mergers and acquisitions.

A company's M&A integration story is usually crystal-clear to executives. And for good reason. Months leading up to an M&A transaction, the entire executive team eats, sleeps and dreams about the transaction and the implications associated with it. They are well-versed in the strategic rationale, business value, cultural implications and customer impact. However, what most executive teams don't do is translate that knowledge into a clear, compelling and consistent story that is meaningful and relevant to employees, partners and customers.

This creates a very real and significant gap between the executive team and the rest of the organization. During the M&A integration process, it's easy for leaders to "assume" everyone knows what they know. But let's be clear, they don't.

Having a clear, consistent M&A integration story that permeates the newly combined cultures and customer experience is so important. A story that translates the "transaction" into messages that are relevant and meaningful to employees, partners and customers.

It is important to note that executives only get one chance to shape the story. And that opportunity comes long before the first day the "transaction" is revealed to an internal audience. The story must be shaped well ahead of this event. The story must be formulated from the point of view of each audience that will be impacted. It must address critical questions and provide these stakeholders with a sense of clarity and confidence in the path forward.

An M&A integration story usually answers questions like these for key stakeholders (employees, partners, customers):

> What was the strategic rationale behind this transaction?
> What does it mean to our business and brand?
> How does it impact me short term?
> What does it mean long term?
> What is going to change?
> What's not going to change?
> What are we supposed to communicate to employees and when?
> What are we supposed to communicate to partners and when?
> What are we supposed to communicate to customers and when?

> How does this event impact the vision, mission and values of the company?
> How does this impact our corporate messaging, positioning and value proposition?

These and so many other questions must be answered and then used to shape a story that creates clarity inside and outside of the organization.

This story must find its way into a sustained, structured and strategic communication plan that breaks down the story into consumable chapters that are shared with stakeholders at specific stages of the integration process. Starting on Day One and continuing through Day 365.

An M&A integration story is the most often overlooked and underutilized lever in the merger or acquisition process. No wonder lack of clear, consistent communication is one of the main reasons M&A transactions fail to deliver lasting value.

Maybe that is why an article in *Europe Business Review* stated, "A successful merger or acquisition comes from carefully combining employee engagement programs with a multi-layered strategy built around communication. With this at the center of the overarching strategy, organizations will have a better chance of bucking the merger and acquisition trend."

As a C-suite executive, make no mistake about it, your M&A integration story matters.

How well you answer these questions, crystallize your messaging and deliver an intentional story inside and outside of your organization will directly impact the ROI you will attain from your M&A transaction.

M&A Communications: Experienced Professionals and Processes Required

There is a reason most companies don't have a full-time M&A integration communication team on staff. The reason is you only need those resources and expertise when you need it. But make no mistake about it: when you need it you absolutely must have it.

With that said, you don't just snap your fingers and assemble an experienced M&A integration communications team utilizing existing, internal resources. You can't just pull people from the organization and expect them to have the scars, lessons learned, expertise and proven processes required to design and implement an effective M&A communications strategy. Why? Because these people have day jobs. You hired them to run specific areas of the business, not to be M&A integration communication experts.

No executive in his or her right mind would take a multi-million, sometimes multi-billion dollar, business initiative and ask inexperienced leaders to attack it on a part-time basis.

Or task leaders with defining a highly complex and intricate strategy when they have no track record of success in that area. It would be like asking your marketing team to step in and implement your new network security system or having your IT team define and execute your annual sales and marketing strategy.

Yet, this is what happens in many M&A transactions. Executives scramble to assemble a cross-functional team to define, manage and execute a communication strategy in support of the M&A integration process. They layer M&A communication strategy, planning and execution on top of the day jobs of inexperienced leaders across the organization. This is a recipe for disaster.

Executives who have gone through mergers and acquisitions understand how critical battle-tested M&A communications expertise is to a successful integration process. They don't put this highly strategic and visible initiative at risk by passing off M&A integration communication to leaders who can only address it on a part-time basis.

Industry research shows that 75 percent of M&A integration challenges are created by communication problems. These include unclear messages, gaps in communication and ill-advised communication plans — internally and externally.

If you want your integration process to run smoothly and the transaction to deliver a maximum return, you need to take your communications strategy seriously.

The only way to do that is to engage a partner that has the proven resources, expertise, tools and processes it takes to ensure the M&A integration process is a success. There are four things you need to look for in this strategic communications partner.

1. **Battle Scars:** If you don't want to make rookie mistakes, make sure your partner has "been there and done that" when it comes to M&A integration. You need to benefit from the lessons they have learned over multiple transactions. You should benefit from the scars they have earned from designing and executing integration communication strategies that did and did not work in the past. You should ask for — and they should be willing to share — real war stories that illustrate the lessons they have learned.

2. **Repeatable Tools:** M&A integration communication requires structured and sustained execution. The right partner can show you the tools and techniques they deploy to engineer and manage a disciplined strategic planning and implementation process.

3. **Disciplined Processes:** Speaking of process, the right partner will have defined processes that they use to drive discovery, development and execution of the integration story and communication plan. They should have documented steps to guide leaders through each phase of the M&A integration journey. Bottom-line, they should be able to show you what a successful messaging and communications roadmap looks like.

4. **Negotiation Skills:** This last requirement is critical. They must have experience working directly with the C-suite and functional leaders across complex organizations. Why is this important? Because this experience will ensure the partner knows how to navigate and diffuse political and organizational challenges that will crop up throughout the integration process. They will be seasoned negotiators, mentors and coaches. They will know how to forge and foster the executive relationships and buy-in that are required to execute a winning plan.

Remember, 75 percent of M&A integration challenges are rooted in communication. Communication problems quickly translate into business problems — negatively impacting employee engagement, organizational performance, customer retention and, in the end, profitability.

Don't put your transaction at risk. Secure the integration communication expertise and resources you need to drive optimal organizational performance throughout the entire M&A integration process.

Culture Isn't Part of the M&A Integration Game, it is the Game

Lou Gerstner, former CEO of IBM Corp., once said culture isn't just one aspect of the M&A integration game, "... it is the game."

So, if culture compatibility, assimilation and integration is so critical to M&A success — why don't more executives take it seriously and put it at the top of their M&A priority list? And, why is it that:

> **More than 50 percent** of executives who execute mergers or acquisitions rarely or never conduct formal cultural assessments?

> **Only 4 percent of executives** include culture-specific questions in their due-diligence checklist?

> **Just 2 percent of organizations** contract with an outside firm to conduct a "culture gap analysis" or compatibility study? (Source: Pritchett Survey)

In most mergers and acquisitions, culture integration seems to fall to the bottom of the list, assigned as a sidebar project and delegated to HR or other business unit leaders to figure out or stumble through.

This is a recipe for failure. Why? Because, if the two workforces don't figure out how to work well together and deliver collective value, the M&A transaction will be a bust. Sure, on the surface, the companies may appear to have similar business models and strategies. Core beliefs may even align. But that's not what culture integration is about. It's about making people (individuals, workgroups, teams) feel like they are part of something new. It's about creating a lasting connection between employees and your newly combined company.

Without a concerted, strategic plan for bringing the two organizations (people, not processes) together — transaction value will quickly diminish. There are three things executive teams can do to ensure this does not happen:

1. **Get Out in Front:** Conduct a deep and wide culture assessment. Know what makes both organizations tick, and identify the gaps / differences that exist. Let the employees know that their voice matters and that you have a plan for bringing the two cultures together. Assess primary concerns and questions. Gather insights that will help you communicate with them and keep them engaged.

2. **Get the Message Right:** Based on the insights gathered from your research and assessment, formulate a story that will resonate and connect with different dimensions of the workforce. A singular vision and purpose is critical, but the story must also be aligned with the specific worlds different stakeholders live in. For instance, what, how and when you communicate to sales may be different from the message you send to technical teams. A singular consistent message, tailored in a way that is relevant to each stakeholder group and delivered at intentional times throughout the process, is a critical element to successful culture integration strategy.

3. **Strap them in for the Long Ride:** Make sure you recognize that this trip will require sustained effort and investment. You will need to allocate the resources and budget to the culture integration initiative. This investment will go toward internal communication programs, executive travel, local events, employee feedback systems and other

efforts that are required to manage the culture integration process. Remind the team that this will be at least 12- to 18- months. So, make sure the team is prepared to stay the course.

It's important to note that mergers and acquisitions also represent an opportunity to reassess and realign your company's vision, mission and values system. This provides everyone with the opportunity to start with a clean slate and begin operating from a new, shared playbook.

In the end, your goal is to create a high-performing culture.

This can only be accomplished when the executive team is committed to shaping and aligning shared expectations, beliefs and behaviors across the newly combined company. And this will only happen when the C-suite makes culture integration a priority before, during and long after the transaction takes place.

CHAPTER 4

How CEO Messaging and Communication Impacts Business Results

Most CEOs Would Be Shocked to See What We See and Hear What We Hear

"Most of you would be terrified to see the serious disconnect that exists within each level of your organization."

The firm was speaking about the lack of understanding and alignment across most companies in each of the following areas...

Vision (where they desire to take the organization)

Strategy (the plan to get there)

Story (words and actions employees use to bring the vision and strategy to life)

To impact organizational performance, clarity and alignment must be established between...

> The C-suite and leaders across the organization

> Line-of-business leaders, managers and frontline employees

> Marketing teams and the customer experience

> Sales representatives and customer conversations

As an executive, you might ask, 'Does organizational clarity and alignment really matter?' We think so.

Here are three real-world examples of how lack of clarity and alignment in these areas has negatively impacted business performance.

1. The C-suite had spent six months communicating a go-to-market strategy that included three growth initiatives. Yet when we surveyed line-of-business leaders in the organization to capture their sales and marketing priorities ... the growth initiatives never even surfaced.

2. A CEO had been communicating the company's vision for more than a year. However, when we asked employees in a workshop how the vision impacted their daily work activities, they said it really didn't.

3. At the beginning of the year, the executive team had defined and communicated three core markets and offerings they wanted to focus on. Yet when we audited the company's sales enablement tools and digital content ... only 20 percent of it aligned with the opportunities they were trying to pursue.

As an executive, ask yourself ...

> How can we hope to attain our vision if employees don't see how it plays a role in their daily work activities?

> How can we achieve our growth initiatives if leaders don't operationalize them in the field?

> How can we attack defined market opportunities if the story we are sharing in the market doesn't align?

Now, these may seem like simple issues to solve. And if that was all there was to it — they would be. However, symptoms such as these usually represent larger clarity and alignment challenges in areas such as leadership accountability, internal communications, corporate culture, operating models, sales compensation plans and marketing strategies.

For some executive teams, this comes as a positive surprise, and they welcome the idea of surfacing and addressing barriers that prevent the company from achieving a higher level of performance. Other executives are looking for a quick, cosmetic fix, and they quickly lose their appetite for what it will really take to achieve greater organizational alignment.

Which camp do you fall into?

No matter how you answer this question, just remember that establishing alignment between your vision, strategy and story is hard. Operationalizing it is even more difficult. However, executive teams that make it a priority and stay the course ... improve employee engagement, increase customer retention and create high-performing businesses.

Don't Allow this Disconnect to Interfere with Business Performance

Ask most C-suite executives if their company's vision, mission, values, strategy and story impact business performance and they are sure to say ... "Well, of course."

However, when you look at how these critical dimensions are managed, you would question just how important executives think they are to business success.

To start with, in most cases these initiatives are developed and managed in silos.

> Human Resources most often maintains the vision, mission and value system across the company.

> C-suite and business executives define and drive the company's strategy and core business initiatives.

> Marketing or corporate communications typically owns the corporate story.

In addition to being managed separately, they also operate on different timetables.

> Vision, mission and value systems are often put aside and only updated when major changes in the business take place.

> The go-to-market strategy may have a two-to-three year shelf life, but most companies launch new strategic business initiatives on an annual basis.

> The corporate story is refreshed sporadically as new agency partners are brought on board, market conditions change or competitive threats arise.

Combined, distributed ownership and inconsistent timing of when these initiatives are refreshed can negatively impact business performance.

Why? Because they quickly get out of alignment. As a result, they no longer drive clarity and connectivity across the business ... they create confusion and doubt.

For instance:

> The company's go-to-market strategy no longer aligns with the vision and mission.

> The corporate story being shared externally and internally no longer supports the go-to-market strategy.

> The leadership team's actions and decisions no longer align with the corporate values.

When these cornerstones of a company's culture and customer experience get out of alignment, employees, partners and customers question their validity and importance. Worse yet, it makes the executive team look misaligned and their message less than authentic.

Don't let this happen to your company.

Form a cross-functional team that is responsible for establishing and maintaining alignment between these critical dimensions of organizational performance. Commit to an intentional process where this team audits, refines and realigns these critical dimensions of organizational performance on an annual basis.

Companies that maintain alignment between their vision, mission, values, strategy and story win.

They win ... because they establish clarity in the minds of employees, partners and customers.

They win ... because they create a unified culture.

They win ... because they deliver a superior customer experience.

It's Time to Get Serious About Pull-Through and Activation Strategies

Maybe there was a day when the CEO or members of the C-suite spoke and those messages were amplified up and down the organization. Well, if there was such a time, those days are long gone.

The noise level inside companies today is louder than ever before. Thus, making it more difficult for executives to get messages that matter to stick and ultimately have a lasting impact on business performance.

That's why it is time for C-level executives to get serious about communication pull-through and activation strategies.

What is that? It's the disciplined and sustained process that ensures strategic messages are heard, embraced and ultimately acted upon at every level of the organization.

Think about it. How detailed, disciplined and sustained was your pull-through and activation process when you rolled out strategic corporate priorities this year? What about your new brand promise? What about changes in the company's go-to-market strategy?

If you're like most executives, you gathered top-tier leaders from across your organization and shared this message with them at an event or meeting. From there, you assumed leaders would passionately and consistently share that message through-out their area of the business. Maybe you even sent out a company-wide email. Well, having worked with large, complex organizations for more than 15 years, we can tell you ... this doesn't cut it.

The message ... is NOT communicated correctly.

The message ... is NOT shared persistently.

The message ... is NOT acted upon by frontline employees.

The message ... does NOT deliver desired business results.

This doesn't mean your leaders are incompetent. It means they are busy. It means they need help. It means they must have the communication tools, air cover and support it takes to deliver the message in a way that it sticks.

As an executive, that's your job. You have to ensure there is a disciplined, persistent communication pull-through and activation strategy in place to ensure critical business initiatives a re a success.

What does a pull-through and activation strategy include?

There are five key components:

1. **Story:** Time and energy are invested to formulate and crystallize a clear, compelling message.

2. **Sequence:** A communication roadmap ensures the story is compartmentalized into bite-size chunks and delivered in an intentional and highly sequenced manner.

3. **Strategy:** A plan targets and tailors the message for relevant roles and areas of the business.

4. **Structure:** A disciplined communication cadence ensures the message is heard, internalized, understood and activated by all critical stakeholders.

5. **Statistics:** A method is created for measuring absorption, retention and activation in specific areas of the organization.

In today's noisy, constantly changing, high-speed business environment, you have to realize that critical messages don't cascade … they don't translate into action … they don't impact business results … without comprehensive communications management.

So, if you want strategic messages to get across and your corporate initiatives to be a success, you need to have a pull-through and activation strategy in place. You need a partner with the communication expertise and methodologies required to engage and activate employees in a way that positively impacts business performance.

Keys to Converting CEO Messages into Desired Actions and Outcomes

This is a message CEOs need to hear over and over again:

There are two keys to translating executive communication into action:

1. Strategic Intent
2. Persistence

Many executives are perplexed when their message doesn't translate into action. They are dumbfounded by the lack of retention that exists up and down their organization. Most executives feel like they have communicated the same message over and over again and it still does not translate into the desired action or outcomes.

Many times, this is because they are communicating the exact same message ... over and over again. Their messaging strategy is one-dimensional. It is not aligned with the learning and adoption curve that is required to translate words into action.

For your message to convert into desired actions, you must communicate in phases. You need to deliver the message with the strategic intent of moving your audience from:

> **Context:** What is this about and why is it important?

> **Understanding:** What does it mean for the company, our customers, etc.?

> **Internalization:** How does this impact me and why should I care?

> **Application:** How do I apply this in a meaningful and relevant way in my job?

> **Operationalization:** How does this change the way my team operates moving forward?

The core message remains constant; it is simply wrapped in a story that is intentionally designed to move your employee from one phase to the next. And, just to be clear ... no, you can't move your audience through the learning and adoption curve by addressing all of these in one long message.

This leads us to the second key to success. Persistence.

Most executives underestimate the sustained communication effort required to translate a message into consistent action. Whether it pertains to changes in the business model, new offerings or strategic initiatives, most CEOs are communicating messages that are critically important and many times complex.

That's why you must realize that your employees are inundated with messages every day ... from every direction.

Persistence is the only way you will get your message across.

Some believe the "Rule of Seven" applies. You have to deliver a message seven times before the desired behavior is activated. However, Microsoft recently conducted a study designed to measure the optimal number of exposures required for audio messages to stick. The study showed that messages must be communicated between six and 20 times to achieve the desired result.

No, this doesn't mean simply sending out one to two messages for each phase of the learning and adoption curve is the answer (2 messages x 5 phases = 10). It means you utilize the repetition and frequency that is required to move your audience from one phase of the adoption curve to the next.

For instance, providing your audience with context may only require one to two messages. However, establishing understanding may require two or three; internalization may require three or four, application eight to 10; and operationalization may demand 10 to 20.

Many factors come into play with respect to communication repetition and frequency. The complexity of the message, the hierarchy of your organization, the number of unique audience segments you must reach and the measurable results that are actually being attained.

So, the next time you plan to activate strategic initiatives, share critically important messages or change the mindset of employees across your organization, ask yourself:

> Where is my organization on the learning and adoption curve?

> What is my strategic intent with this particular message?

> What repetition and frequency are required?

The key to success is anchoring your communications plan in strategic intent and persistence. Only then will your words translate into the actions and outcomes you want to see in the business.

CHAPTER 5

Voice of the CEO and C–Suite: A Defining Factor in Organizational Performance

CEOs Don't Just Own Strategy. They Own the Story Behind It.

If an organization succeeds or fails at implementing corporate initiatives, navigating a crisis, completing a merger, launching a new product line, or living up to the company's vision, mission and values ... the CEO is accountable.

Why? Because he or she owns the strategy. And not just the business strategy — the messaging and communication strategy that is required to make it a success.

Sure, C-suite executives hold themselves accountable for strategy. However, what many executives have not acknowledged is they own the story behind it.

In a recent article published by Wharton School of Business, communications expert Walter G. Montgomery said:

"CEOs commonly blame lousy communication when well-laid plans go awry. Yet, paradoxically, communications is an undervalued, lightly regarded discipline in the theory and practice of corporate leadership."

Think about how much brain power and energy you and your C-suite put into shaping strategic business initiatives.

Now, think about the small amount of time (in comparison) you spend on the messaging and communication strategy in support of it. As a C-suite executive, you may not be the one to actually put words on paper (many do), but you absolutely need to lead, shape and guide the messaging and communication strategy that is used to bring the strategy to life. No one knows the business strategy like you do. No one knows the story behind it like you do. You need to be involved throughout the entire journey.

Montgomery went on to say...

"Chief executives need to focus on communications as a management capability more seriously than they typically do. They should lead a thorough rethinking of what communications does and should do, subsequently transforming it into the constructive force it can be."

Modern CEOs are taking Montgomery's advice.

> They know, if communication breaks down, business performance goes down.

> They realize business strategies, when backed with the right messaging, deliver better results.

> More importantly, modern CEOs know they have to own the process because, at the end of the day, success or failure lies on their shoulders.

Winning business strategies are driven by successful messaging and communication strategies.

So, if you're a CEO or C-suite executive, it's time to redraw the boundaries around strategic communication in your business, placing yourself and members of your C-suite squarely in the middle of it.

Great CEOs Are Consistent, Persistent Communicators

Great CEOs and C-suite executives never underestimate the power and influence their message can have on the business.

They realize a crystal-clear message — that generates strategically aligned decisions and actions — is what separates high-performing companies from the also-rans.

However, most CEOs underestimate what it takes to formulate a message employees truly embrace and the work required to convert that message into desired business results.

Great CEO communicators don't make this mistake.

They spend a significant amount of time working with experts to formulate their message. They get outside counsel to ensure that message is relevant and resonates with stakeholders up and down the organization. They also put control mechanisms in place to ensure the message does not get diluted as it filters its way through the organization and into the customer experience.

One of the great CEO communicators was Jack Welch, retired business executive and former CEO of General Electric. Like him or hate him, he knew how to convert a message into action. In the book, "Jacked Up," the author describes how Welch took the time to review every senior-level presentation his top team delivered at the company. Some would say he did this because he was a control freak. However, great CEO communicators see the genius in this disciplined action.

Welch put this process in place to make sure his message was understood by leaders, translated correctly and delivered consistently up and down the organization. Great CEO communicators realize this is just one of many control mechanisms they must put in place if they want the message to manifest itself into desired business outcomes.

A recent *Harvard Business Review* article said, "Understanding the importance of being understood is what makes great CEOs great communicators." However, in today's always-on, noisy and hyper-connected business world, being heard (much less understood) has become extremely challenging for CEOs. That's why CEOs must be extremely intentional about formulating and managing their message. To do this, they need to get outside counsel, put rigorous processes in place and follow a disciplined cadence.

Ultimately, as the CEO, if you want strategic initiatives to translate into business results — you must put strategic message development, delivery and management at the top of your priority list.

Is this a priority for you? Let's see. What's your message around the company's ...

> Fiscal year business priorities?

> Primary market or customer opportunities?

> Latest organizational change initiative?

> Recent merger or acquisition?

> Vision, mission, values and culture?

If none of these are relevant, pick one of your top initiatives.

What message are you delivering to ensure its success? Do leaders understand the message? Are they translating it correctly and consistently? Is that message driving desired actions from frontline employees? Is your message positively impacting business results?

The *Harvard Business Review* article I referenced earlier went on to say ...

"... if people can't constructively enhance and advance the CEO's essential message inside the enterprise and out, then something is profoundly wrong with either the people, the message, or the CEO."

Are your strategic initiatives being operationalized in a consistent, comprehensive and effective manner?

If not, does the blame lie on your people? Your message? Or, the fact that you have not yet put all the pieces in place for you to become a great CEO communicator?

More CEOs Need to Speak Their Minds

This may sound counterintuitive and go against everything happening in the world today, but CEOs and C-suite executives need to speak their minds.

They need to deliver the message they know must be received to drive change or improve results at their companies. The reality is, this is not happening today.

The world we operate in is so hypersensitive, over-filtered and politically correct that the voice of the CEO and C-suite has been diluted.

The CEO's message has lost its authenticity. It has lost its power. And more importantly, it is losing its impact on business performance.

In most organizations, CEO and C-suite messages are getting watered down, dumbed down and filtered to the point where they no longer serve their original purpose: to move the organization forward and in a very specific direction.

We see this every day. Too many cooks in the kitchen. Too many so-called experts in the room watering down the recipe. Too many stakeholders across the business adding their preferred ingredients. By the time the message leaves the boardroom and finds its way into the organization, it no longer serves the original strategic intent. Your job is to deliver a message that matters and makes a difference ... not make everyone happy. Maybe that's why world renowned researcher and author Michael Porter said:

"Strategy 101 is about choices: You can't be all things to all people."

As the CEO or a C-suite executive, you are being paid to make a choice.

The choice about what message needs to be communicated to move the business forward. You must ensure that unfiltered message accomplishes its strategic intent up and down the organization. Even if that isn't the story others would like to hear or tell.

In the book "Good to Great," Jim Collins said executives are responsible for getting ... "the right people on the bus, the wrong people off the bus, and the right people in the right seats."

Your message in support of critical business initiatives should do just that.

Especially when it comes to messages that are intended to move the business forward. Like your message around vision, mission, go-to-market strategy, culture, brand, positioning, and organizational change.

You don't need translators. You don't need filters. What you need are the right messengers who will deliver the right story to the individuals you want on the bus. With that said, many executives lean on outside counsel to ensure the right story (their story) comes together without non-value-added interference.

An advisor who understands their business and their strategy can capture the story in the voice of the CEO and package it in a clear, compelling and consistent way. Not someone who gets hung up on a creative way to spin the story — but a trusted advisor who will ensure the strategic intent behind the story is ultimately achieved.

If you're a CEO or C-suite executive, it's time to take back control of your message.

It's time to speak directly to your constituents in your true voice. No more filters. No more translators. Just a true, authentic message that you genuinely architect and intentionally deliver to move your business forward.

What Is Your
C-Suite's Story?

Twitter, Slack, Chatter, LinkedIn … the business world we operate in today is driven by instantaneous communication.

Employees, partners and customers now have immediate access to the messages being delivered by your organization. And the message starts at the top. So, what's the story coming out of your C-suite?

As a C-suite executive, it's time to acknowledge that the new currency in the digital age of business is communication. The ability to develop, deliver and activate a crystal-clear message will define market leaders and laggards in the future.

C-suite executives must embrace this fact. You can no longer ignore the impact strategic messages have on business performance and the technologies that are changing how those messages are delivered. Any inconsistency or crack in the armor can negatively impact employee engagement, brand reputation, customer retention and, ultimately, the financial performance of the business. That's why the voice of the C-suite is more critical than ever before.

Modern executive teams get this.

They are investing the time and resources required to formulate strategic C-suite messages that matter and leverage innovative technologies to deliver that story across their organization and into the marketplace. These executives understand that before they can leverage technology in a positive and meaningful way, they first must define the stories they have to tell. The messages that must get through to employees, partners and customers.

As a C-suite executive, ask yourself ... what are the stories we have to share? What messages do we need to champion and manage over time? What messages will ultimately determine the success of our organization?

Is your team on message? Can your C-suite answer the following questions with absolute clarity and alignment ...

> What's the story behind our brand and purpose?

> What's the story behind our go-to-market strategy?

> What's our culture and employee recruitment story?

> What's the story behind our current organizational change initiative?

> What's our story to current and prospective investors?

C-suite teams that spend time defining these strategic messages and ensuring there is a pull-through and activation strategy behind the story — will outperform their competitors.

And a critical part of the pull-through and activation strategy is the cadence by which the C-suite actively participates in the communication process. How they leverage the latest communications technology on a consistent and intentional basis to ensure the message is delivered precisely when and where they want it.

Are you active on Twitter? How is this channel being used?

Are you leveraging enterprise messaging technology like Slack to engage leaders across the organization?

What about LinkedIn to communicate with partners and customers?

Are you intentionally using these technologies to explain and reinforce strategic messages that must get through to positively impact business performance?

Communication pull-through and cadence should be part of every C-suite meeting. It should become a cornerstone of how your team operates month to month, quarter over quarter. The goal is to actively manage a consistent, sustained cadence by which each C-suite executive supports and delivers strategic messages through the technologies that matter most.

The days of delegating strategic, organizational communication to others are over. C-suite executives must take the reins — like they once did years ago.

Why? Because only those executive teams that make strategic messaging development a priority, define sustained pull-through strategies and leverage innovative communication technologies will succeed at engaging employees, partners and customers in meaningful ways. Ways that ultimately drive business and financial performance.

CHAPTER 6

Clarity (or Lack Thereof) and Its Direct Impact on Business Performance

Your Employees and Customers Crave Clarity

As we work with executive teams around the world, it is amazing to see those who get it and those who don't.

What is ... it?

It ... is the direct connection between organizational clarity and business performance.

So, we are going out on a limb here to say, without question, **the number one priority for every CEO is establishing and maintaining clarity.**

Clarity in purpose.
Clarity in strategy.
Clarity in culture.
Clarity in story.

Employees need it. Customers demand it.

Yet, with that said, we still see many executive teams paying little attention to these dimensions of organizational performance. In fact, more often than not, this is the degree of C-suite involvement we see in each of these areas.

Purpose
Most executive teams invest the time to conduct a "find our purpose" workshop and define a purpose statement. Then they

hand the keys to the head of internal communications to handle the rest. Many believe their job is done.

Strategy
This is an area where executives spend a significant amount of time, yet they spend very little effort formulating a plan to ensure the strategy is infused into the minds of employees across the organization.

Culture
Culture raises its head when things get ugly, like when employee retention or recruitment numbers aren't looking so good. Otherwise, defining, managing and maintaining culture gets relegated to HR.

Story
This is the message that defines the position the company wants to own, what it does, what makes it different and the value it delivers. This becomes a priority for many executive teams when competitors are threatening their market position. Otherwise, this story changes with the wind and is delivered inconsistently by sales and marketing professionals across the organization.

We are not trying to disparage or be disrespectful to C-suite executives ... after all they are our clients. They are our reason for being. We are just being honest.

The truth is, very few C-suite teams pay enough attention to purpose, strategy, culture and story. You could say this isn't their job — they have lieutenants who are responsible for these things. We would beg to differ.

At the high-performing companies we have worked with, C-suite executives made an intentional decision to apply sustained effort across all four of these dimensions. Not only shaping and defining what they are, but also working to ensure they are infused into the minds of employees and customers. Why? Because that is what it takes to establish and maintain clarity.

The most common excuse we hear from executives, as it relates to the minimal time they spend in these areas, is they are soft and hard to measure.

But the simple fact is clarity translates into improved business performance.

It just does.

In fact, the Institute for Public Relations (IPR) conducted an extensive, global research project to answer the question 'Does organizational clarity drive organizational success?' The study discovered there was, in fact, a direct correlation between the degree of clarity across the employee population and the company's overall performance.

Does your organization have the clarity it needs to drive optimal business performance?

Do Your Employees Even Know What Your Strategy Is?

It is amazing to see the breakdown that exists in most organizations. More specifically, the communication breakdown relative to a company's go-to-market strategy.

When you survey leaders, managers and frontline employees at most organizations, many of these critical stakeholders do not even know what the company's go-to-market strategy is. Let alone, how the strategy pertains to their daily work activities.

> In fact, research conducted by Metrus Group discovered that only 14 percent of employees understand the organization's strategy, and less than 10 percent of all organizations successfully execute the strategy.

Strategies are only effective when they are executed — and executed consistently. The cornerstone of effective execution is awareness and understanding. This can only be achieved through persistent and consistent communication of the strategy.

More than anything else, business performance is negatively impacted from poor communication of strategy. And a significant shortfall in business performance today can be directly attributed to lack of "communication accountability" up and down the organization.

Who owns communication accountability — especially as it pertains to strategy?

The CEO and C-suite. Period.

Modern CEOs are quickly acknowledging this. In fact, in the study, "Communication from the CEO's perspective – an underestimated challenge?" CEOs surveyed said they believe...

Communication has itself become part of the strategy and therefore a core business management function in its own right.

So, while Gartner has long projected that companies will compete based on "customer experience," we believe that the competitive battle will be fought and won by those companies that achieve and maintain organizational alignment in support of a clearly communicated strategy.

Now, don't confuse simply having a strategy with achieving success. After all, almost every company has a strategy.

Only those CEOs and C-suite executives who take the time to document, translate and communicate that strategy over a sustained period of time will win.

A study conducted by FTI Consulting reinforced the connection between strategy and communication. It discovered that high-performing organizations establish and maintain intentional connections between the individuals who develop the strategy, those who manage the strategy and, ultimately, those who execute the strategy.

The key word is intentional. This means if you want your go-to-market strategy to translate into flawless execution, you must intentionally craft a message around the strategy that is relevant and meaningful to those who manage and execute it. This also means you must have intentional communication processes in place to ensure that message gets through.

While results from FTI's most recent study did find that, year over year, CEOs have increased the weight they place on communication — it also clearly illustrated that communication of the strategy remains a problem.

The study still found that a major cause of failed strategies continues to be a lack of understanding and support from key constituencies. What this means is most CEOs and C-suite executives are not placing enough energy, resources and time behind the communication initiatives required to foster awareness and understanding of their strategy.

Do you want to win? Do you want your strategy to materialize into measurable results? It's time to elevate communication on your priority list. It's time for you and the entire C-suite to ensure every employee has a deep, meaningful connection to your go-to-market strategy and how it impacts their job.

The Lost Art (and Science) of Sustained Executive Communication

We live in a world of instant gratification. Do something fast. Do something once. Expect immediate and lasting results.

What a joke.

What's more concerning is that this instant gratification mindset has crept into organizational communication, and it is killing business performance.

Sure, CEOs and C-suite executives are moving so fast, you rarely have time to catch up on email. You have so many balls in the air, you touch each one for about 5 minutes — each week, each month. I get it. Your world is complicated. Your business is moving faster than ever. You have more and more people pulling at them every day. This is just the reality for every CEO and C-suite executive.

However, we have worked with business leaders at Fortune 100 and high-growth companies around the globe for more than 15 years. And we have discovered one thing separating executives who lead high-performance, focused organizations from others. When it comes to organizational communication, they don't buy into instant gratification.

They are intentional about the messages they send and how those messages are communicated up and down the organization.

Simply put, they stay the course because they know firsthand the impact intentional and sustained communication has on business performance. More importantly, they know that nothing less will actually deliver lasting results.

No matter how busy or complicated their worlds are, these executives are very focused on delivering sustained messages that matter. Messages that drive clarity, alignment and execution. Messages that pertain to ...

> Brand promise and purpose
> Vision and mission
> Culture and employee engagement
> Organizational change
> Strategic business priorities
> Customer experience

When it comes to messages that matter, these executives ensure the story is omnipresent. Not just through their own communication but within the communication that comes from every leader across the organization.

This reminds me of a Fortune 100 client that recently made a sizable investment to bring more than 200 leaders together for a strategy meeting. During the meeting, a new set of strategic priorities were shared. Strategic priorities that had to be activated across the organization for the company to achieve its annual revenue targets. Keep in mind, while there were 200 leaders in the room, the company has tens of thousands of employees around the globe.

Now, those executives who live in the world of instant gratification would leave the kickoff meeting patting themselves on the back. Mission accomplished. The strategy was communicated. The initiatives were clearly laid out. Their job was done.

However, executives with a "stay the course" mentality would acknowledge that their work had just begun. To translate the priorities into meaningful action, an intentional communications plan had to be activated. Not for a few weeks, or even a couple of months, but for a sustained period of time. Enough time for thousands of employees across the organization to convert these high-level concepts and priorities into action and, ultimately, measurable results. Now, these leaders would leave the meeting with a sustained communications game plan. They would stay the course.

CEOs and C-suite executives often forget: Communication that drives results in large organizations is like turning the Titanic. It takes time before the ship starts to move in the direction you want it to go.

So, don't let the instant gratification world we live in distract you from staying the course. Buck the trend. Be an intentional, sustained communicator and you will outperform your competitors every time.

CHAPTER 7

Top–Performing CEOs Make Organizational Communication a Priority

When Was the Last Time You Truly Looked at Your Story?

Business is moving at light speed. Changes are happening inside and outside of your organization faster than ever before. Yet, when was the last time you stopped down to really evaluate your corporate story? The story that is supposed to communicate who you are, what you offer, why you are different and where your company is going?

As a CEO or C-suite executive, can you honestly say, without a doubt, that your company's...

> Value proposition is still relevant based on changes in customer requirements and buying behaviors?

> Positioning is still aligned with your go-to-market strategy and vision for the company?

> Story is complete even with the changes and additions that you have made to your products / services portfolio?

> Key points of difference are still ownable given the current competitive landscape?

As a CEO or C-suite executive, it's your responsibility to ensure that the answers to these questions are undeniably "Yes." You own the company story. No, not just the story you share with Wall Street or the investor community — but the one that is shared with your customers. The story your frontline employees, sales organization, digital properties, content marketing and social channels are delivering in the market every day.

Jack Welch, retired business executive and former CEO of General Electric, was infamous for reviewing all of the presentations his leaders delivered across the organization. He did this for a very good reason. The business was constantly evolving and the story had to keep pace. It had to stay aligned with the company's vision and strategy if it was to pull the business forward. And to ensure the message was being delivered consistently, he made it a priority to stop down and ensure alignment started at the top.

We need more CEOs like Jack who are strongly committed to delivering a consistent and fully aligned corporate story.

Based on our experience, the message being delivered by most companies trails far behind the strategy C-suite executives are focused on executing.

The story no longer supports desired positioning based on where the company is today ... let alone where it is headed. The story doesn't align with the buying preferences and behaviors of the company's current and desired target audience. It is no longer a differentiated story based on changes that have transpired in the competitive landscape.

This is a problem. Why?

Because today, more than ever, your corporate story is omnipresent in the customer experience. It is the one thing that is always on and being consumed 24 / 7. If this story is not aligned with your company's go-to-market strategy and vision — you will not win. If it does not connect with what your target audience truly cares about — you will not win.

You've probably heard this statistic over and over again: "prospects are almost two-thirds of the way through the buying process before they even talk with someone at your company." How does this statistic relate to the topic we are discussing? Well, it means that the majority of a customer's selection and buying decision is now based on what?

You guessed it — your corporate story and messaging.

CEOs must make clear, compelling and strategically aligned corporate messaging a priority if you want to win.

You must create intentional stop downs once, if not twice a year, to fully audit and bring your company story into alignment with your vision, mission, strategy and customer requirements. You must answer questions like ... is our current story complete and accurate? Is it crafted in a way that will enable us to achieve our desired business objectives? Is it designed to engage and connect with customers who will control our future success?

Here's the bottom line: CEOs and C-suite executives who develop and deliver a corporate story that is intentionally designed to pull the company forward will win more customers and become leaders in their respective markets.

Realize What Truly Drives High-Performing Organizations

Studies show that most CEOs separate culture initiatives from their business strategy and story. Actually, culture is the byproduct of your story and strategy in action. The words and actions of every employee embody your company's story and strategy.

CEOs and C-suite executives must understand that words matter. You must acknowledge that the message behind the company's story and strategy play a significant role in the type of culture that takes root inside your business.

So, the real question here is, what is the state of your go-to-market story and strategy? How clearly and consistently are they communicated up and down your organization?

One way to find out is by answering the following questions...

Do our employees understand the company's story?

> Our company's purpose?
> How we want to be positioned in the market?
> Who we are?
> What we do?
> The value we deliver?
> What makes us different in the market?

Do our employees understand our strategy?

> Vision?
> Mission?

> Values?
> Customer needs and desires?
> Promise to customers?
> Pillars of our go-to-market strategy?

Executives who answer these questions with a resounding "yes" will most likely have high-performing cultures. Executives who answer "no," or don't really know the answers to these questions, need to understand that lack of clarity is negatively impacting their culture and business performance.

The fact is, CEOs who produce winning cultures maintain complete clarity and alignment between their story and strategy. They also ensure that their entire employee population understands, internalizes and activates the company's story and strategy in daily work activities.

Your story and strategy ... create a shared mindset.

When employees have a deep understanding of what your company stands for, what it does and how it creates value for customers, their purpose becomes clear. They feel more connected. They believe what they do matters. Clarity of purpose is a powerful motivator. And, it's born from a clear, compelling and consistent corporate story that aligns with your go-to market strategy.

Your story and strategy ... drive aligned actions.

When leaders and team members across the organization understand how the strategy connects with the story, congruent actions and decisions unfold. Your company's vision, mission and values go beyond words on paper and take on a life of their own. Employees see how strategic decisions, investments and initiatives connect with the story. They understand how their marching orders align with the bigger picture. For this to happen, leaders must ensure the story and strategy are consistent and omnipresent.

Clarity and connectivity are the keys to a high-performing organization.

When your story and strategy are clearly defined and documented — and fully immersed in your company's culture — magic happens. As research from Duke University states ...

"An effective culture is like an invisible hand at work inside of each of the employees that helps to guide their decisions and judgments in a way that the overall corporation would desire it to be."

Culture is formed when consistent words and actions, aligned with the corporate story and strategy, are constantly on display — when what is expected and what is acceptable become second nature to each employee. Everyone seems to operate from the same sheet of music. Which is why one executive who participated in Duke University's research said, "Culture is your sheet music to success. It is no different than an orchestra. You can hire the best trumpet players, oboist, violinist, and unless they are all playing from the same sheet of music at the right tempo, you will fail. If you have the trumpets playing too loud, the song won't sound right. It is that delicate balance of getting people on the same page."

Do your employees have the clarity they need to perform at the highest level?

The problem is, most C-suite executives and business leaders are not providing employees with the same sheet of music. As a result, employees lack clarity — clarity around what the company stands for, how it differs from the competition, and what its greater purpose is. They also lack clarity around the story the company needs to tell in the market and the promise it needs to make to customers.

Without clarity around the company's story and strategy, there

is nothing for the employee to connect with. There is nothing shared from department to department or division to division.

When it comes to maintaining organizational clarity, one executive interviewed by Duke University said it best:

"A good leadership team and good CEO will put in the processes to make sure the message filters down to the very bottom of the organization unchanged."

The key word here is unchanged.

CEOs who want to establish high-performing organizations must understand it all starts with a clear, consistent corporate story and strategy. Then they must ensure that story and strategy is infused throughout their employee population.

Anchor Messages
to Combat Change
and Create Clarity

Product and service innovation, customer requirements, competitive movement, digital transformation, mergers / acquisitions ... the pace of change is increasing on every front in business.

As a result, many CEOs and C-suite executives feel like firefighters. Constantly adjusting strategies and messages based on prevailing winds shifting from minute to minute.

The job of a C-suite executive is not to fight fires. Instead, the CEO and C-suite's job is to establish anchors for the organization in a world of constant change.

More specifically, they are responsible for setting clear expectations for what will not change; what will remain true and constant — no matter what, irrespective of changes going on inside and outside of the business.

What are those anchors? They are the messages that:

> Describe the heart and soul of the business

> Differentiate the brand

> Distill what the company stands for

> Define customer experience expectations

Often, these anchor messages get pushed aside when the company is going through rapid change. It's all about the here and now. It's all about daily tactics and firefighting. The sad thing is ... this is precisely the wrong thing to do. Because when the storms roll in, employees and customers need to call upon those anchor messages.

They need to be reminded of what matters most and the things that aren't changing. They need to connect with messages that define the foundation of the business. Messages that will guide how they react to change and make decisions that are in the best interest of the business — long term.

When competitors are knocking at their door, when customer service issues crop up, when technology fails, when product delays occur ... that's when "anchor messages" matter most. That's when these messages directly impact business performance.

Executive teams that have established and communicated clear, compelling and consistent anchor messages can weather any storm. They can get through the daily fires and still deliver superior business results. Those that have not ingrained these messages into the hearts and minds of employees and customers cannot.

> Do your employees and customers clearly understand your company's purpose?

> What about your brand promise?

> Do employees embody your core values?

> Do employees and customers understand what differentiates you from the competition?

> Do they have a firm grasp of your vision?

Only when employees and customers have knowledge of and belief in these anchor messages can they rise above daily distractions and disappointments — and remain loyal and true to your business. Anchor messages create a sense of stability and clarity around what matters most long term. They relate to your company's purpose, mission, values and promise to customers. They relate to your customer experience goals and long-term strategy.

As we work with executives around the world, we often see these anchor messages posted on breakroom walls and in brochures throughout the buildings.

Rarely do we see them come to life in the words and actions of the employees walking the halls. But when we do — it is noticeable.

There is clarity and calmness in the air. There is clear, intense focus in their eyes. They recognize that trials and tribulations will rock the business, but they know the executive team has positioned the company to rise above it. Employees are able to stay focused on the things that matter.

They understand that while products and services, business processes, technology, competitive pressure and other aspects of the business may change — the most important things will not. Those are the anchor messages that create clarity and alignment — up and down the organization — even when fires pop up from week to week, month to month and quarter to quarter. They rise above the flames and focus on solutions that align with the company's anchor messages.

As a CEO or C-suite executive — you need anchor messages that guide and shape the beliefs and actions of employees and customers. You need to ensure those messages are ingrained in their minds so that when change occurs and all hell breaks loose ... they instinctively grab hold of what matters most.

CHAPTER 8

Redefining Corporate Communications Success in the C-Suite

CEOs Who Increase Organizational Clarity Improve Business Performance

Ask most C-suite executives if their company's vision, strategy, culture and story matter and they will say, "Of course they matter." But the real answer is uncovered when you ask the next question …

"What are you doing to ensure clarity and alignment exists in these areas — up and down your organization — on a consistent basis?"

In most cases, their answer is vague and delivered with less conviction. So, let's be clear: Having a vision is one thing. Infusing it into the fabric of your culture is another. Defining your go-to-market strategy is one thing. Translating that strategy into a message employees can understand and activate is something else.

The truth is, many business leaders are amazed to learn that **70 percent (7 out of 10) of all employees are unknowingly misaligned with their company's strategic direction and just 55 percent of middle managers can even name one of their company's top five priorities** (*Harvard Business Review*).

These executives are even more shocked when they hear that **90 percent of their frontline employees don't know what their company stands for and what makes it different from the competition** (Gallup).

Bottom line: In the rapidly changing business environment we operate in today, organizational clarity and alignment doesn't happen by chance.

What degree of clarity and alignment exists across your organization?

The first step in improving organizational performance is to understand the degree of clarity and alignment that exists across the company. This is accomplished by conducting a thorough assessment of the four dimensions of organizational performance:

Vision: Your reason for being, your purpose, the dent your company wants to leave in the universe.

Strategy: Your macro go-to-market strategy, core business initiatives and priorities.

Culture: Shared mindset, behaviors and actions across the business.

Story: Your company's positioning, value proposition and promise to customers.

The assessment enables you to understand how aligned the organization is around the shared beliefs, decisions and actions that are required to drive optimal business results.

How do you get started?

Quantitative Research

Online surveys can be used to assess clarity in all four areas across your entire employee population. Quantitative survey results are compiled, analyzed and segmented. You should be able to analyze the results with a high degree of granularity so you can pinpoint high-performing and low-performing areas within the organization.

Qualitative Research

Extensive one-on-one interviews are also conducted with a cross section of your employee population. Interviews are conducted across every functional area of your business and at multiple levels (executive, middle management and individual contributor). During these interviews, we cover all four dimensions of organizational performance, surface valuable performance insights and identify obstacles that may be preventing you from attaining greater clarity in various areas of your business.

Findings and Recommendations

After your discovery work is complete, you will need to analyze the findings and formulate recommendations for your executive team. The findings should be shared with your executive team in a formal presentation. During this meeting, you will also want to share specific recommendations for improving clarity and alignment within specific areas of your business.

Your Corporate Message Matters More than Ever

I hate to say it, but many of today's CEOs have lost touch with a critical fact in business: The strength of a company's story is intrinsically tied to the financial performance of the business.

You get out of it what you put into it.

If your corporate story is ineffective and inconsistently delivered … financial performance suffers. However, when your story is clear, compelling and consistently delivered throughout the customer experience … top-line and bottom-line results thrive. Why do I believe many CEOs have lost touch with this fact? How else can you explain the lack of strategic time, energy and investment the C-suite puts into the development and delivery of a consistent corporate story?

Most companies treat corporate messaging as nothing more than words on paper.

Most companies develop and deliver their corporate story in an ad hoc manner.

When you take those two facts and add that we work in a business world driven by instant gratification, short cuts and quick wins … you have a recipe for disaster.

Here is your CEO wake-up call.

The development and delivery process matters.

Tactic-driven, inconsistent and isolated — this is how most companies approach the development and delivery of their story throughout the customer experience. If your corporate message is going to drive financial performance, your messaging development and delivery process has to matter, and the CEO needs to send that message loud and clear up and down the organization.

It must be strategic, intentional and holistic.

Remember, your message is not an ad, it's not a slogan, it's not even the message on your website. It's the story that is consumed throughout the customer journey: across all channels and every touchpoint. Yet, why is it that many C-suite executives look for the quick win when it comes to getting their message in the market? You launch new campaigns, new annual reports, websites … and think your work is done. You wonder why financial metrics aren't moving in the right direction.

To be honest, I don't think you truly believe these tactical things are going to materially impact customer acquisition, retention and loyalty — but I do think you forget what will actually deliver results.

Infusion and activation determine ROI.

Even if a company lands on an extremely compelling message, if it's not consistently delivered throughout the customer journey, it won't be the story customers take away from the experience they have with the business. That's why CEOs and C-suite executives have to redefine what the finish line looks like. It's not landing on a clear, compelling and consistent message.

That's just the starting line. If executives want their corporate story to have a material impact on the financial performance of the business — a clear, compelling message must be infused

throughout the customer experience. That means the message must be activated inside and outside of the organization. **A customer experience awakening is required.**

Just a few years ago, making sure stakeholders (beyond the marketing department) understood the corporate message was a luxury — a nice-to-have. It is now a business imperative. Why? Because today, the customer experience is the battleground on which business is won and lost. The customer experience is made up of so much more than just a new website or campaign. It takes a village to deliver a clear, compelling and consistent corporate message throughout the entire customer journey. In the modern business world, it takes unwavering executive-level commitment (time, resources and investments) to ensure every stakeholder who plays a role in the customer experience is able to bring a consistent story to life.

Customer behavior has changed ... have you?

Too many CEOs are still living in the past. They don't understand that the rules of engagement have changed. They are not willing to fundamentally change how they approach messaging development and delivery — inside and outside of their organization. My only caution to these executives is this: beware. In the past, repercussions of delivering a fragmented, disconnected message in the market may not have jumped off the P&L. But that's because the way customers engaged with and consumed your story was different. Make no mistake about it ... it's a new world and it's an entirely different competitive environment. Your message matters more than ever before.

CEOs and C-suite executives who hang onto the old-school approach to corporate messaging development and delivery ... will lose. Those who change the way they bring a clear, compelling and consistent story to life throughout the entire customer experience ... will win. And win big.

So, if you want a new ad campaign — have at it.

However, if you want to make a material impact on top-line and bottom-line financial performance, be prepared to lead the way and invest in a disciplined corporate messaging development and infusion process across every customer-facing part of your business.

Your Legacy Mindset Regarding Marketing Has Got to Go

In the business world today, the customer has taken center stage. That means CEOs and C-suite executives must change the way they think about marketing's role in the enterprise. They must reset the boundaries and expand marketing's reach into and influence over the entire customer experience. Gone are the days of marketing's sole focus being brand awareness, generating leads and launching campaigns. They have been replaced with a more holistic ownership of the customer journey.

It's time to redefine marketing's role across the organization.

CEOs have to lead the charge when it comes to changing the way executives across the enterprise view marketing, how it operates and the degree of control it has over the customer experience.

Simply put, marketing should be defined and confined only by the customer journey itself.

With this fact in mind, leading CEOs are starting over. They are clearing the slate and using the customer journey as the foundation from which they task marketing with developing strategic plans, formulating budgets and building the brand.

According to McKinsey & Company, "Few senior-executive positions will be subject to as much change over the next few years as that of the chief marketing officer. Many CEOs and boards may think that their senior marketers' hands are already full managing the rise of new media, the growing number of sales and service touchpoints, and the fragmentation of customer segments. But as the forces of marketing proliferation gather strength, what's actually required is a broadening of the CMO's role. This expansion will encompass both a redefinition of the way the marketing function performs its critical tasks and the CMO's assumption of a larger role as the voice of the customer across the company."

CEOs must lead the charge and open new doors.

While some CEOs and executive teams may not have the appetite for this reset — it is the right business and financial decision in the long run. In fact, CEOs who redefine marketing's role in the business, with customer experience at the center, will ultimately gain and maintain greater market share than their competitors. However, to make this happen — you, as the CEO — must be prepared to drive change.

For your CMO and marketing team to be successful, you will need to ensure they can capture greater knowledge of the customer through analytics; have more involvement in the formulation of your company's go-to-market strategy; take on broader messaging development and delivery responsibilities; and have the authority to lead customer-centered initiatives that span almost every functional area of the company.

In other words, you will have to completely redefine, in the minds of leaders across the organization, where marketing's job starts and stops.

Yes, you will need a strong, strategic CMO ... but you must have their back.

A recent Forrester article, "CMOs Boldly Reach for More Influence in the Enterprise," explains that, "CMOs should step forward and take responsibility for turning the enterprise toward the customer. This means taking on a more significant role on the executive team ... it also begs CMOs to lead innovation processes in the organization ... the CMO, has to create a more engaged customer relationship. Getting the organization to see the CMO in this light is a big ask, and only CMOs who rethink their approach to marketing operations will pull it off."

With that said, as the CEO, you must have the courage and persistence to lead the way. Your marketing leaders can't do it themselves. To win, the entire executive team must commit to working with marketing to re-center the business around the customer experience.

In fact, a recent Heidrick & Struggles study found that 62 percent of CMOs view relationships with peers on the senior executive team as vital to their success. We think that percentage should have been closer to 100 percent. Why? Because without philosophical and strategic alignment between the CEO and CMO and unwavering commitment from the C-suite to transform marketing — companies will experience limited success in the future. It's just that simple.

CHAPTER 9

How CEOs Capture the Customer Experience Opportunity from the Inside Out

In the Experience Economy, There's No Place to Hide

Fact: The always-connected customer has unprecedented access to your organization.

C-suite executives need to realize that how their business operates, what their organization believes in, the actions their employees take and the messages used to describe their business are omnipresent. These messages and interactions define the employee and customer experience with your company. They also represent the new competitive environment that C-suite executives must contend with today.

What does this mean for the C-suite? Business transparency, employee engagement and the customer experience demand complete alignment between your company's words (story) and actions (strategy).

It means your company's words and actions matter more than ever before.

The words you use and the actions you take define how employees and customers perceive their experience with your company.

While your strategy drives desired actions, your message drives the storyline these critical stakeholders experience throughout their journey with your company. That's why your story and strategy must be fully aligned. When they are not, the employee and customer experience breaks down. The perception of your brand is damaged. Employees and customers lose faith and trust in your company. And worst of all ... they leave and go to the competition.

Achieving clarity and connectivity between your story and strategy.

A recent article in the *Journal of Business Strategy* stated...

"In its simplest sense, a corporate story is a narrative tool that tells the tale of a company's strategy in action. It is a clear, structured, compelling articulation of 'who we are' and 'where we're headed' that rallies emotional and rational support from stakeholders."

The article goes on to say ...

"More than mere words, however, the corporate story's strength lies in its ability to align leaders, drive decision making and mobilize the organization."

That's why every stakeholder involved in the employee and customer experience must deeply understand how your story and strategy connect.

Your corporate story gets stakeholders to instinctively activate desired words and actions.

As a C-suite executive, it is your job to ensure that the corporate story and strategy are embraced at every level of the organization. This means every employee should be able to communicate with conviction: Your company's higher purpose, core go-to-market strategy, the value your company delivers and your promise to customers.

However, for this to happen, C-suite executives must lead the charge. They must secure unwavering commitment from the entire leadership team to infuse shared beliefs and behaviors throughout the employee population. This is accomplished by designing and implementing a sustained internal organizational change initiative that ensures every employee can instinctively activate the company's story and strategy as they engage with customers ... and one another.

Does it really matter?

C-suite executives who maintain alignment between their corporate story and strategy will deliver a superior employee and customer experience. And as a result, they will reap the rewards that they secure from increased employee and customer acquisition, retention and loyalty.

In fact, according to Bain & Company, "Great customer experiences produce great business results. Look at companies such as Apple, Costco, American Express, Philips and Allianz. Different industries, different business models. But they have one thing in common — large and growing groups of passionate customer advocates, earned by delivering an experience competitors can't match."

14 Changes Every CEO Must Contend with to Win in the Experience Economy

If you're a CEO or C-suite executive, it has taken you awhile to get to where you are in the organization. So, it's probably safe to say that a significant amount of time has passed and a lot of changes have taken place in the business world since you were on the frontline.

Since then, some of the most significant changes have been in customer buying behavior, the sales process, marketing strategies, self-service technologies and communication channels. All of which have changed the way companies must go about engaging and converting prospects to customers.

As a C-suite executive, it's always a good idea to stop down and take a hard look at how these changes should be driving changes in your business. Changes in your go-to-market strategy, culture, sales efforts, marketing investments and what it takes to compete and win in the "experience economy" you operate in today.

Here are 14 changes that every C-suite executive must contend with to experience success in the future ...

1. YESTERDAY: Marketing "controlled and pushed" the corporate message out into the marketplace through defined channels.

TODAY: Your message is actively consumed by prospects and customers 24 / 7 / 365 from any and all communication channels.

2. YESTERDAY: Sales reps were the primary way customers got to know your company.

   TODAY: Customers experience your products, services and story without human intervention — when, where and how they wish.

3. YESTERDAY: Marketing's biggest priority was acquiring leads.

   TODAY: Marketing must not only focus on securing new business, but also play a significant role in how your company retains, grows and increases loyalty among customers.

4. YESTERDAY: Brands were built through controlled campaigns, channels and messages.

   TODAY: Brands are defined by the words and actions customers experience across unlimited touchpoints.

5. YESTERDAY: Employee communication and engagement with the customer was limited, contained and controlled.

   TODAY: Customers communicate and connect with your employees through numerous channels and methods every day.

6. YESTERDAY: Product features and functionality were the basis of differentiation.

   TODAY: Products are commodities — the end-to-end experience customers have with your company is now the battlefield of differentiation.

7. YESTERDAY: Sales reps controlled their pipeline and qualification process.

   TODAY: The self-service buying process puts the customer in control — they can opt in or out before the sales cycle even begins.

8. YESTERDAY: Shifts and changes in your business strategy were not immediately visible to customers.

   TODAY: Misalignment between leadership and the frontline is immediately recognized and damages customer acquisition, retention and loyalty.

9. YESTERDAY: Executives were the only thought leaders and voice behind the brand.

   TODAY: Every employee has a voice on the web and impacts brand perception and loyalty — every day.

10. YESTERDAY: Corporate message consistency was controlled by marketing through traditional campaigns.

    TODAY: Your message must be managed and delivered consistently across the entire employee population, sales and marketing partner ecosystem, as well as online and offline communication channels.

11. YESTERDAY: Employee engagement was a given — they worked for a paycheck.

    TODAY: Employees want to work for a higher purpose and understand the role they play in your company's purpose and story.

12. YESTERDAY: Customer loyalty was achieved based on the strength of very few, trusted relationships.

   TODAY: Customer loyalty is based on minute-by-minute, day-by-day experiences with every team member and technology platform that enables each step of the customer journey.

13. YESTERDAY: Poor customer experiences and stories about your business were contained.

   TODAY: Negative messages and stories can be shared with the world anytime … anywhere.

14. YESTERDAY: Alignment between your corporate story and strategy was critically important at the leadership level.

   TODAY: Customers expect the words and actions of every employee to align with your corporate story and strategy.

With all of these changes, CEOs and C-suite executives must recognize that customer engagement and communication strategies from the past are a recipe for disaster in the future. Forward-thinking executives will take time to reconnect themselves with the realities of the business world today. They will evaluate and ensure their company's go-to-market strategy, culture and business processes align with the experience economy — so they can compete and win for years to come.

Barriers Preventing CEOs from Delivering a Consistent Story Throughout the Customer Experience

As a CEO or C-suite executive, it is critical that you think about one simple fact: Today, your prospects and customers have unlimited access to your business. Their experience spans more people, processes and technologies than ever before. This has resulted in an explosion in the number of ways prospects and customers interact with your company. The greatest impact of this explosion has been felt in three key areas:

Organizational structure: There are more individuals and teams that have customer-facing communication ownership and responsibility within the enterprise than ever before. Think about all the customer-facing areas of your business and the interactions they have directly or indirectly (via technology) with your customers every day.

Communication channels: Never before has there been more channels through which companies communicate with customers and through which customers communicate with companies. From websites to social channels, customer portals, online chat and email, the list goes on and on.

Partner ecosystem: Technology has had a dramatic impact on the number of sales and marketing partners companies must manage. A few years ago, a single agency may have handled the majority of how, when and where the company story was told in the marketplace. Today, companies have dozens of partners developing and delivering messages at distinct points in the customer experience.

These changes become more difficult to contend with when you add barriers that have been constructed throughout your organization:

Distributed ownership: The number of individuals, teams, partners that are responsible for developing and / or delivering the corporate story throughout the customer experience has dramatically increased.

Functional silos: The independent functions / roles within departments, business units, divisions and partner ecosystem that communicate and engage with customers has grown significantly.

Multi-channel integration: The sheer number of channels and communication vehicles used to communicate and interact with customers has exploded. The complexity of integrating and synchronizing all these channels can be daunting.

All of these changes, combined with barriers that have been formed over time, have had a tremendous impact on how companies develop and deliver their story.

Visualize how your story is told today.

Take a moment to paint a customer-facing picture of your organizational structure, communication channels and partner ecosystem. Look at each of these through the lens of how your corporate story is developed and delivered throughout the customer experience. Which areas of your organization interact with the customer? How many communication channels are being utilized to connect with prospects and customers?

Which partners play a role in each dimension of the customer experience? If you are like most CEOs, the picture you see includes:

> Highly distributed ownership of messaging development and delivery internally and externally.

> Functional silos across the business that interact with customers on a consistent basis.

> Limited connectivity between a wide range of technologies and communication channels used in each phase of the customer experience.

Regain control over the story you are delivering.

Ultimately, this picture illustrates the very real and growing complexity that you must contend with if you want to develop and deliver a consistent corporate story throughout the customer journey. Ask yourself:

"Do I really have disciplined, enterprise-wide processes in place that will ensure our organization delivers a consistent story throughout the customer experience?"

If you are honest, the answer is probably no. And that's OK. Currently, most executive teams don't have the disciplined processes in place to break down these barriers and ensure that a consistent story is told throughout the customer experience. However, those executives who address these barriers and deliver a consistent story reap significant rewards.

In fact, a recent McKinsey study revealed the No. 1 trait of companies that succeed in delivering a superior customer experience is the ability to develop and deliver a clear, consistent corporate message. That's why if you want to establish competitive differentiation based on customer experience, you must deliver a consistent story across all three phases of the customer experience (self-service, sales and post-purchase).

The story your customer consumes can no longer be ignored. The simple truth is, CEOs and C-suite executives can no longer ignore the enterprise-wide messaging development and delivery problem that exists within their companies. If you are serious about organizational clarity, alignment and performance, and if customer experience is a true priority for your executive team ... then it's time to apply the discipline, energy and resources required to break down these barriers. It's time to put intentional processes in place that will ensure your company is well-positioned to deliver a clear, compelling and consistent story throughout the entire customer experience.

10 Commitments CEOs Must Make to Experience Success

For the customer experience to translate into improved financial performance and serve as a competitive advantage, it must be embraced enterprise-wide. It must be implemented in a cross-functional manner. And, it has to be a priority for you and your entire C-suite.

Here are 10 commitments you must make, as the CEO, if you want to experience success ...

1. **Commitment to a Customer-Driven Culture and Strategy**
   First and foremost, you must make customer centricity a cornerstone of the company's business strategy. You must be committed to driving customer knowledge deep into the fabric of the company's culture. A superior customer experience can't take shape without your commitment to securing and sharing rich, actionable insights about your customer. This commitment should take the form of increased funding in support of customer research and knowledge-sharing systems.

2. **Commitment to Customer Experience Ownership**
   If you are committed to creating a customer-centric culture and institutionalizing the customer experience as a cornerstone of the company's business strategy, ownership must be clearly established and defined. You should appoint a sole leader of customer experience management who can be fully responsible for defining, managing and optimizing the customer experience. This individual must be equipped with the authority to manage across organizational and political boundaries and be empowered to influence or enact change.

3. **Commitment to Direct C-Suite Reporting Relationship**
   With an executive-level owner in place, you must formalize a direct reporting relationship with the C-suite. Ideally, this individual would report to you. However, this is not a requirement. What is required is a direct reporting relationship to a C-level executive and direct access to the executive team. Why is this critical? Because it's imperative that the customer experience leader ensure executive business decisions are aligned with customer requirements and vice versa.

4. **Commitment to C-Suite Involvement and Funding**
   Each member of the C-suite must play an active role in shaping the customer experience strategy. Finance, operations, marketing and other functional leaders must be held accountable for actively managing customer experience initiatives that pertain to their area of the business. Performance metrics and budget dollars that pertain to C-suite areas of responsibility should also be assigned. This is the only way you can enforce accountability and the customer experience leader can secure executive-level time and attention.

5. **Commitment to Cross-Functional Leadership Accountability**
   Active C-suite involvement must go beyond the boardroom. You and your C-suite executives must hold lieutenants accountable for leading initiatives that are designed to improve the customer experience. Leaders must understand the strategic nature of customer experience initiatives within their area of the business. They must realize these initiatives and the associated business results will be visible at the highest level of the organization. Not momentarily, but over a sustained period of time.

6. **Commitment to Organizational Change (People, Process and Technology)**
   You must ensure everyone in the organization embraces changes that are required to deliver a superior customer experience. You need to make it absolutely clear that there are no sacred cows, that political motivations are outlawed

and that functional barriers are being torn down. You should constantly remind everyone that it's all about the customer and about delivering a consistent experience. In addition, your customer experience leader must have complete autonomy and authority to inject change into customer-facing areas of the business.

7. **Commitment to Crystal-Clear Performance Metrics**
A critical part of customer experience management is securing agreement on the customer experience metrics that matter. What business performance improvements are we in search of? What specific dimensions of the customer experience do we need to improve? What metrics will we use to measure the results? Once customer experience metrics have been defined, your job is to get every member of the C-suite to lock arms and communicate that these are the KPIs we are focused on. This is the data set that you will be using to monitor and determine what is working ... and what is not.

8. **Commitment to Measurement and Reporting Systems**
Securing commitment on performance metrics is only half the battle. You must get the C-suite and leadership team to implement data collection, measurement systems and reporting processes so you can capture and act on those insights. Your team should implement systems that will provide you with visibility and access to the metrics that matter at every level of your organization. The key to success is prioritizing and starting small. Don't overcomplicate things. Start gathering metrics that require the least amount of lead time and disruption. This will enable you to start surfacing meaningful data early in the process.

9. **Commitment to a Realistic Timeline for Business Impact**
The most critical factor in achieving success is ensuring executives are fully aligned with respect to timing. More specifically, when do you expect customer experience management to materialize into business results? Do you expect business results to come next quarter? Next year?

Two-to-three years down the road? Setting time-to-impact expectations across the executive team is critical. When expectations are out of alignment, uncertainty and doubt creep in and commitment quickly becomes compromised.

10. **Commitment to Sustained Customer Experience Cadence**
    The final commitment you need to make pertains to the cadence of communication and management of your overall customer experience initiative. You need to ensure the strategic importance and business value of customer experience remains omnipresent. This is important because the only way to change the corporate culture — and ultimately the customer experience — is to ensure customer-centricity is woven into the fabric of the company. You, your C-suite, business unit leaders, directors and managers must follow a consistent cadence by which changes, progress and results are captured and shared.

All 10 are non-negotiable — if you want customer experience to be a difference maker.

If you want customer experience to deliver material results, these are non-negotiable. You and your entire C-suite must be willing to stand behind these commitments if you want to compete and win in the experience economy.

CHAPTER 10

Employee Buy-in and Customer Buying Requirements Have Changed. Has Your Business?

Employee Actions and Words May Be Killing Your Business

CEOs and C-suite executives must realize that the actions taken and the words used by their employees directly impact the customer experience and the company's financial results.

So, as a CEO or C-suite executive, how can you influence those actions and words? It's simple.

Your corporate strategy should drive consistent actions and outcomes across your organization.

Your corporate story should drive a consistent storyline throughout the customer experience.

With that said, to deliver consistent financial results and a compelling customer experience, your corporate strategy and story must be fully aligned.

Why? Because you can't do one thing and say another.

When this happens, trust is broken. Your employee and customer experience breaks down. Brand perception is damaged. And that's how employees and customers lose faith and belief in your company.

How do you avoid this from happening?

You get serious about your strategy and story. More specifically, you get serious about driving alignment around your strategy and story — up and down your organization. Executives must be committed to ensure employees can instinctively and consistently activate the company's strategy and story as they engage with customers and one another.

What does it require from you to make this happen? Alignment between your strategy and story.

Executive Team and Leaders
Your entire executive team must be fully aligned with your go-to-market strategy and story. This requires having a clearly defined corporate purpose, vision, mission and values system in place. The executive team must also crystallize the core value your business delivers, what differentiates your company from the competition and the key messages that will connect with your customers, employees and partners. We recommend that you develop a unified Corporate Strategy and Story Platform that will serve as the foundation for planning and decision-making across the business.

Frontline Employees
Employees crave clarity. Clarity increases their commitment and conviction in what the company does and what it stands for. You must have programs in place that ensure every employee fully understands and internalizes the corporate story and strategy. This dramatically improves employee engagement, loyalty and productivity. It also ensures they play a positive and active role in bringing a consistent story and strategy to life in the customer experience.

Internal Communications
The message you deliver internally must be aligned with the company's go-to-market story and strategy. The executive team must put disciplined processes in place to ensure internal communication plans and programs align with the company's purpose, vision, mission and values. Processes also need to be in place to ensure the corporate strategy cascading down from leaders to managers and frontline employees is clear and consistent.

Human Resources

It is imperative the messages you are sending to employees are fully aligned with the messages they are being asked to share with customers. Executives must work with the HR team to ensure the corporate strategy and story being shared with prospective and current employees is fully aligned with external messaging, from recruiting materials to onboarding presentations and employee engagement programs.

Public Relations

Executives must ensure the PR team is leveraging a consistent, enterprise-wide corporate story to formulate media strategies, pitches and stories. This will help you keep media briefings, interviews and coverage on message. The public relations team, internal subject matter experts and PR firm also need to fully understand and be able to communicate the company's strategy across a wide range of public relations activities.

Investor Relations

Investors demand consistent and predictable results. The same is true when it comes to the company's story and strategy. The executive team must ensure the corporate story and strategy being shared with investors is fully aligned with the messages being communicated throughout the customer experience. Greater consistency and alignment in the strategy and story increases investor confidence in the executive team's ability to execute and own a differentiated position in the market.

Marketing

Marketing is responsible for delivering a consistent story and promise across critical communication channels utilized throughout the customer experience. The executive team needs to ensure marketing fully understands how the strategy and story connect to daily work activities. With a documented corporate strategy and story in place, marketing teams can ensure continuity and connectivity exists from one customer touchpoint to another.

Sales

Executives must ensure the sales team's voice is aligned with the corporate strategy and story. This will ensure a consistent value-based message is delivered in selling conversations and that the message aligns with the story buyers consume throughout their end-to-end journey. Disciplined processes must be put in place to ensure sales fully buys into the corporate story and can articulate the strategy in a clear, compelling way.

Partners

Your partners play a vital role in the customer experience, and today companies have larger partner ecosystems than ever before. That's why it is imperative that your partner ecosystem is operating from a shared corporate strategy and story. This will create greater connectivity and continuity in the messages partners deliver across various channels, communication vehicles and touchpoints throughout the customer experience.

As a CEO and C-suite executive you might be saying, "I have lieutenants who are responsible for these areas of the business." That is true. However, if they don't have access to a shared corporate strategy and story — how can they operate from the same sheet of music? If they have not been educated on how the strategy and story relates to their area of the business, how can you expect their teams to execute effectively on a daily basis?

It's no wonder industry research has indicated less than 15 percent of employees understand what the organization's strategy is, and almost all frontline employees don't know what their company stands for. They have not been given a consistent roadmap to operate from nor have they been told how to navigate it.

Do you want to outperform
the competition?

Do you want to deliver better
bottom-line results?

Then you better get serious about aligning
and activating your corporate story and
strategy across your organization. And
remember, as a C-suite executive, while you
may not own the end-to-end execution
of your strategy and story ... you sure
own the activation plan behind it.

Achieve Success Through Consistency, Connectivity and Continuity

In the hyper-connected, always-on, customer-driven world we operate in today, leading CEOs are leaving their old-school definitions of marketing and communications behind. They are writing a new playbook. A communications playbook for the entire enterprise that is rooted in delivering a consistent, connected and cohesive story throughout the customer experience.

Consistency serves as the cornerstone.

As a CEO or C-suite executive, you have long understood that formulating a meaningful and relevant corporate story is critical to success. However, what you may not have realized is that delivering a clear, consistent story throughout the customer experience ultimately determines the winners and losers in business today.

In fact, I would go so far as to say that a flawed, less-than-compelling corporate story — delivered consistently throughout the customer experience — will outperform a highly effective, relevant message that is delivered inconsistently every time.

Connectivity is what establishes critical links.

One thing successful companies have been known for is launching things. Launching new brands. Launching new campaigns. However, what will define successful companies in the future is not how well they launch things ... but how consistently they link things. More specifically, intentionally linking the various conversations, communication channels, marketing vehicles and touchpoints that play a critical role in the customer journey. An article on Business2Community.com crystalizes this thought:

"Customers don't need more ads, emails, eBooks, webinars, workshops, phone messages, sales meetings ... they need an experience that turns their interest to purchase. You must think about every touchpoint in a very intentional way rather than simply creating yet another marketing initiative."

Continuity is about the customer experience.

The customer experience serves as the battleground for the business connectivity and continuity of your story like never before. To be successful, CEOs are deploying an entirely different approach to managing the corporate story throughout the customer journey. They are reengineering roles, responsibilities and processes. They are reaching across "party lines" and developing connected, cross-functional messaging development and delivery processes between every customer-facing area of the company. CEOs are breaking down silos across the business that prevent the company from delivering a clear, consistent and connected story. They are demanding the development of cross-functional communication strategies and implementing change management programs to transform how the company's story is brought to life throughout the customer experience.

Why is consistency, connectivity and continuity so important to the modern CEO?

Because, the customer experience has fundamentally changed how prospects and customers engage with your company. It has also changed the way companies acquire, retain and create loyal customers. These changes are sweeping and impact almost every facet of the business.

Leading CEOs are meeting these challenges head-on by redefining how their organization delivers the company story. They are designing and implementing messaging development and delivery processes that will meet the communication and connectivity requirements of today's buyer.

In the end, leading CEOs are transforming their companies into customer-centric organizations that are intentionally engineered to bring a clear, compelling and consistent story to life throughout the customer experience.

Creating Clarity in the Mind of Your Customer Starts in the C-Suite

To establish clarity in the minds of customers, the C-suite must make corporate messaging a strategic priority across the organization and fully buy into the fact that the story directly impacts the financial performance of the business. It also requires the C-suite get sales, marketing and customer experience leaders in a room to define what the story is and devise a new game plan for how that story will be delivered across all three phases of the customer experience (self-service, sales and post-purchase).

For executives to develop a compelling and authentic message, the corporate story should be rooted in the company's go-to-market strategy, competitive intelligence and insights gained from voices that matter. These voices include prospects, customers, employees and partners. Then the executive team must invest the time and energy to build a holistic corporate messaging platform that will serve as the foundation for customer communication across the enterprise.

This platform must include specific, intentional words and phrases that tell the complete corporate story. A story that captures the essence of the company's:

> Purpose
> Vision
> Mission
> Values
> Promise to customers

> Positioning statement
> What we do
> The value we deliver
> What makes us different

The critical role your story plays in all three phases of the customer experience.

With a strategically aligned Corporate Messaging Platform in place, executives must then work with customer experience professionals and functional leaders to activate the story. The goal is to establish conviction in the story and ensure processes are in place to activate consistent messages across critical channels and touchpoints throughout all three phases of the customer experience (self-service, sales and post-purchase). Let's examine the role each phase plays in the customer experience:

Self-Service Phase
This phase of the customer experience is increasing in importance every day. The self-service phase is where prospects and customers are engaging with your corporate story independently, without any human interaction from your organization. This is where they are learning more about your company, people, products and services predominantly online, consuming content and messages through a wide range of digital channels. According to research by a management company ...

"60% of decision makers start their buying journey with informal research, using search engines and business blogs to research products, problems and solutions."

To reap the greatest value in the self-service phase of the customer experience, you must cultivate engagement and trust, which is accomplished by ensuring that a clear, compelling and consistent message is delivered across critical self-service channels and touchpoints.

Sales Phase

The buying journey is a critical aspect of the customer experience and consists of two distinct, yet highly connected processes: self-service and sales. The self-service phase, as we have discussed, takes place when prospects conduct independent research and consume your corporate story without interacting with anyone at your company. This is when they decide if they want to engage in actual sales conversations. If they like your story, content and point of view, they will engage with a salesperson.

At this point, the goal is to ensure sales professionals are well-positioned to connect with, extend and add to the story consumed during the self-service phase. However, if marketing and sales are not working from the same sheet of music, the self-service and sales experience can break down because of inconsistent and disjointed messaging. That's why it's imperative that marketing and sales are working from a common Corporate Messaging Platform, and why sales enablement tools and selling conversations must be infused with strategic messages from this shared platform.

Companies that connect the self-service and sales phase of the customer experience with a clear, compelling and consistent corporate message spark meaningful and trusted connections and conversations with customers.

Post-Purchase Phase

The post-purchase phase of the customer experience plays a significant role in repeat purchase, customer retention and loyalty. In fact, according to research conducted by New Business Strategies ...

"60 percent of Fortune 500 companies say their purchase decision is based on what the buyer believes their post-purchase experience will be like."

Many executives default ownership and accountability for the post-purchase phase of the customer experience to the customer service or support department. Needless to say, this is a blatant oversimplification. The truth is, almost every aspect of the business plays a role in the post-purchase experience. Sales, sales support, product management, marketing, public relations, account management, and professional services just to name a few. The executive team must get more involved in shaping the post-purchase phase of the customer experience. After all, it is in this phase of the journey when the promises and messages the company has communicated during the self-service and sales process must actually be fulfilled. Purpose-driven brands leverage the power of a consistent story.

The bottom line is, your story shouldn't (can't) change from one phase of the customer experience to the next. The story should become richer, clearer and more compelling as the customer journey takes shape. This reminds me of a great quote in the *Wall Street Journal* from Susan Credle, Global Chief Creative Officer at FCB ...

"The most successful brands are purpose-driven and don't get bored with their story, because it is authentic to them. They retell it over and over again in new, surprising, creative ways. The story doesn't change because of a new CMO or a new agency. The pace might get more dramatic, the plot might take a twist, but it is still the same story."

Are you telling a consistent and compelling story throughout all three phases of the customer experience (self-service, sales and post-purchase)? If you are not, you're missing out on an opportunity to build stronger, more profitable customer relationships that will deliver sustained business growth.

Five Questions Every CEO Must Answer to Maximize Customer Engagement

The number one trait of companies that succeed in delivering a superior customer experience is the ability to develop and deliver a clear, consistent message. (McKinsey)

Today, prospects and customers expect continuity and consistency throughout the buyer journey. One way CEOs and C-suite executives can ensure this happens is to implement a disciplined process for developing and delivering a consistent story throughout the customer experience.

Here are five questions every CEO should answer to determine if their corporate story is maximizing engagement and growth throughout the customer experience.

1. Is your corporate message clear, compelling and consistent? 73% of CMOs indicate that their teams are not on message. (CMO Council)

Most executives think if they have a snappy corporate tagline and value proposition, the corporate story is complete. But the reality is, that will only go so far with respect to engaging and converting prospects to customers. There has to be more to the story. That's why executive teams need to ensure there is a comprehensive corporate messaging platform in place and embraced across the organization. This complete version of your story serves as the foundation for clear, compelling and consistent communication throughout the customer experience. A corporate messaging platform goes well beyond a simple, one-page messaging document for the marketing department. It includes a broad range of actionable messaging content and tools for every customer-facing area of your business and drives messaging continuity throughout the customer journey.

2. Are your employees able to bring your story to life?
70% of brand perception is driven by employees. (Enterprise IG)

To bring your corporate story to life and cultivate lasting change in the customer experience, every employee must buy into and be armed with the key messages that can be delivered consistently across critical touchpoints in the customer journey. From casual conversations over the phone to customer-facing presentations, your employees must be able to deliver clear, compelling elements of the story with every connection they make. For this to happen, executives must ensure formal processes are in place that enable employees to internalize, personalize and activate the corporate story in daily work activities.

3. Are you capitalizing on every customer conversation?
53% of sales executives say that consistent messaging in sales is a significant challenge. (SAVO Group)

In this self-service age of the customer, buyers consume a large percentage of your corporate story before ever speaking with a salesperson. That's why messaging continuity and connectivity is essential between the self-service and sales phases of the customer journey. Executive teams must ensure clear, compelling and consistent corporate messaging is infused into sales tools and selling situations if they want to ignite trusted conversations with buyers and improve sales results.

4. Is your thought leadership strategy aligned with your corporate story?

56% of companies do not have a documented thought leadership strategy. (Content Marketing Institute)

According to the Pedowitz Group, "Content is not a nice to have. It's your voice and direct link to customers and prospects ... companies must make sure it aligns with their marketing message." So, needless to say, thought leadership is critical when it comes to engaging today's buyer. To maximize engagement throughout the buyer journey, your company's content strategy must be intentionally designed to extend and amplify critical elements of your corporate story. This will ensure the story buyers consume from one phase of the customer journey to the next is clear, compelling and connected.

5. Does your story and visual brand align?

While your corporate story is the foundation of business success, it must be wrapped in memorable creative to achieve maximum audience engagement. That's why brand integration — creative execution that is aligned with your messaging strategy — is so important. Your visual brand (colors, images, photography, etc.) must be intentionally designed to bring the corporate story to life if you want maximum engagement throughout the customer experience.

So, are you maximizing the return on every connection you make?

The days of marketing owning the voice of your company are over. Today, every employee and touchpoint a buyer interacts with can make or break the customer connection. That's why your organization's ability to deliver a clear, compelling and consistent message is so important.

Remember, consistency and connectivity in your story won't happen by chance.

As a CEO or C-suite executive, you have to play an active role in the process. More specifically, you must ensure your organization has:

> A corporate messaging platform in place and your story is fully embraced across your organization.

> Intentional processes that are used to deliver a clear, consistent and connected story across customer-facing parts of your business and critical technology-enabled touchpoints.

Only then will your corporate story become a competitive advantage and your business be well positioned to succeed in the customer experience economy you operate in today.

CHAPTER 11

Leveraging Real Customer Insights and Stories to Accelerate Growth

Is Your C-Suite Committed to Activating Real Customer Insights?

"Customers want to talk, and businesses want to listen — but to do so successfully, companies have to overcome the challenges that threaten to drown out the Voice of the Customer." – Questback

As a CEO or C-suite executive, are you serious about listening to and acting on customer insights and feedback?

Do you have intentional processes in place that ensure you stay in touch with the voice of your customer?

In the experience economy we operate in today, having a formal initiative in place to capture customer insights and stories is no longer an option. It's an absolute requirement for doing business.

And in this economy, the only competitive advantage companies have is the ability to deliver a superior customer experience. This reminds me of what Jack Welch, retired business executive and former CEO of General Electric, once famously said ...

"We have only two sources of competitive advantage: the ability to learn more about our customers faster than the competition, and the ability to turn that learning into action faster than the competition."

So, we will ask you again:

Are you serious about listening to and acting on customer insights and feedback?

This quick checklist will assess your executive team's commitment to elevating and activating the voice of your customer across your business. Take a minute to honestly answer these questions:

___ Our C-suite and executive team leverages Voice of the Customer (VoC) insights to drive the way our company's strategy evolves, the way our culture evolves and how we serve our customers.

___ We have defined processes through which real customer insights and stories are captured, packaged and shared to elevate the VoC in our culture.

___ Our leaders have agreed to use real customer insights and stories to consistently increase understanding of and empathy for customers across our employee population.

___ We have identified specific areas of the business that are responsible for collecting, analyzing and acting on VoC insights.

___ We have identified the VoC insights that are captured across multiple dimensions of the customer experience.

___ We have defined how VoC insights and customer experience stories are used to drive daily, monthly, quarterly and annual decisions and strategies in specific areas of the business.

___ We have a process by which we leverage real customer experience stories in the sales process to connect with prospective buyers and grow our business.

Our executive team has agreed upon, and we have documented answers to, the following questions:

____ Why is VoC important to our long-term business success?

____ How will we elevate VoC and real customer experience stories in our culture?

____ How are we going to use VoC insights to improve the way we do business?

____ How will we measure success?

How did you do? The truth is, if you want to compete in today's experience economy, you need answers to these questions.

You also need to ensure that your organization has formal methods through which leaders listen to and act on customer feedback and insights. Why? Because in the future, only those companies that implement a repeatable process for capturing and activating real customer insights and stories will be in the position to deliver a superior customer experience. And only those executives who truly understand and stay in front of rapidly changing customer requirements will survive.

Are You Committed to Voice of the Customer?

Almost every C-suite executive claims that their company is — or desires to be — customer-driven. However, the truth is that very few executives base their business strategy and daily decisions on an intimate understanding of the customer and real customer insights.

Constructing a customer-centric business starts at the top.

If you truly want to leverage Voice of the Customer (VoC), it has to start with you.

For VoC to be a difference-maker, the entire executive team must make VoC a key driver in the business and omnipresent in the corporate culture.

What does it take to make this happen?

What level of commitment is required from you and your executive team?

Let's delve into what it takes to define and manage a winning VoC initiative and find out. But first, let's define what VoC is:

"Voice of Customer is a formal initiative used to gain collective insight into customer needs, wants, perceptions and preferences through direct and indirect questioning. VoC goes beyond just hearing what customers are saying to actually listening, taking what is heard, deriving meaning and intent from that, and turning it into action."

Based on this definition, do you have or are you ready to launch a formal VoC initiative across your business? Before you answer that, let's break down the definition a little further.

A formal initiative

For anything to be considered a formal business initiative, it must have complete CEO and C-suite endorsement and support. It also needs to be comprehensive in nature. This is true for any successful VoC initiative. VoC initiatives must be driven from the top-down and drive improved decision making across multiple dimensions of your business. VoC must be viewed as a foundational element for how your strategy evolves, how your culture is formed and how your customers are served over time.

Gain collective insight

VoC is not one-dimensional. It is not simply capturing customer satisfaction data. To be successful, VoC initiatives must be intentionally designed to capture multidimensional insights from your customer experience and across critical elements of the business. From sales, to product development, user experience, fulfillment / delivery and customer support. What's important is that you identify specific areas of the company that can benefit most from VoC insights and how those insights will be used to improve or change the way the business operates moving forward.

Listen to what customers are saying

Most C-suite executives focus on analytics and business impact too early in the VoC process. They forget that before employees will care about a VoC initiative, they must first understand how their decisions and actions actually impact the customer. For this to happen, they need to hear real stories from the VoC. This means your C-suite must make a concerted effort to elevate real customer experience stories across the organization. Employees must literally see that customer stories are part of your culture. By sharing real stories in daily work activities, employees will start to listen to, understand and empathize with your customers. Remember, they won't care about metrics and data until they care about the customer. So, the entire executive team must be willing to invest a significant amount of time sharing real customer insights and stories throughout the business.

Turning it into action

Only after you have defined how VoC insights will benefit specific areas of the business, demonstrated C-suite commitment and elevated real customer experience stories in your culture can you expect employees to be engaged in the process. With these cornerstones in place you are ready to start analyzing and acting on the data / insights you capture. Now comes the most important part of the VoC process — taking action. You must define specific actions you will take based on the data you are collecting. How will you use VoC insights to:

> Evolve your go-to-market strategy?
> Make user experience improvements?
> Implement customer service models?
> Deploy self-service technologies?
> Refine fulfillment and delivery processes?
> Enhance marketing messages?
> Improve sales strategies?

Deciding how the insights will be used to drive daily, monthly, quarterly and annual decisions and strategies is the final piece of the puzzle. Remember, what matters most is that your employees not only have access to the VoC data but also understand what the insights are telling them to do differently or better.

So, are you ready to commit to VoC?

Before you set sail with a VoC initiative at your company, you and your C-suite executives should answer these questions:

> Why are we doing this?
> What will success look like?
> How will we use the insights to improve specific areas of the business?

If you and your executive team can't align on the answers to these fundamental questions, then don't invest in VoC. You will just be wasting a lot of time and money.

However, if you and your executive team are aligned and committed to applying sustained effort in each of the areas we have outlined — VoC can become a strategic advantage for your organization and deliver a significant return on investment in the years ahead.

How Leading CEOs Increase Customer Empathy and Understanding

If you're a CEO or C-suite executive and you want to create a customer-centric culture, you need to increase two things in the minds of your employees:

1. Understanding of the customer.

2. Empathy for the customer.

How do you do this? Well, you could and should start by formulating a customer-centered business strategy and ensuring that every employee understands how it translates into daily decisions and actions. But that alone won't be enough. Why? Because you are still missing one key ingredient for success:

Voice of the Customer (VoC)

That's right, if you want to create a deeper understanding of your customer and empathy for your customer — employees must hear their voice ... their stories. Real customer experience stories that bring their challenges, aspirations, experiences and outcomes to life in your company. Are real customer stories that important? Well, according to Adam Grant, a professor at Wharton ...

"When customers describe how a company's products and services make a difference, they bring a leader's vision to life in an incredible, memorable way."

By elevating real customer experience stories, as a C-suite executive, you paint a more vivid and real picture of your vision, and your message about creating a customer-centered culture becomes much more credible. In fact, David Hofmann, an organizational psychologist, also said...

"Employees generally see customers as more credible than leaders as sources of inspiration. When leaders attempt to deliver inspiring messages, many employees react with skepticism, questioning whether leaders are just trying to get them to work harder."

By blending real customer experience stories into organizational communication, you create more meaningful connections with your employees. So why don't more CEOs and C-suite executives integrate real customer experience stories into their cultures?

Here are a few reasons ...

They believe stories are soft and have little impact on business performance.

Many executives don't realize that real customer stories do matter, and they do impact business performance. They also don't understand how these stories can dramatically improve the company's culture and customer experience over a sustained period of time. But they absolutely do. In fact, Adam Grant said, "Stories can have a significant, lasting effect on employees' motivation, performance and productivity."

They aren't willing to invest the time and resources required to make it happen.

If you are serious about elevating real customer experience stories in the company's culture, you must make capturing and sharing these stories a priority. And this requires that you invest in a continuous customer story discovery and distribution process. A sustained process that is focused on identifying, capturing and sharing real customer stories internally and externally. For this to happen, you must ensure the following elements are in place:

Ownership: An individual and team (insourced / outsourced) must own customer identification, data collection, story development and activation.

Alignment: Customer stories that are captured and shared should align with and help achieve culture and customer experience goals in critical areas of the business.

Process: The entire process must be defined, documented and repeatable. It must produce a stream of real customer experience stories that are shared on a continuous basis.

Persistence: The initiative must have executive support and involvement. Real customer experience stories must be woven into executive, leader and manager communication.

Ultimately, as a CEO or C-suite executive, you must ensure there is an engine in place that produces real customer experience stories on an ongoing basis. Stories that model the behaviors, actions and outcomes you aspire to achieve.

With this engine in place, you will see how the stories you secure and share begin to blend with stories that organically surface at every level of your organization. And that's how you will know employees have a solid understanding of your customer, empathize with your customer and that your culture is truly becoming customer-centric.

The Impact Real Customer Stories Have on Business Performance

"Despite the marketing rhetoric and self-proclamations of being customer focused, most companies are product centric, not customer centric. Calling yourself customer centric doesn't make it so." — Chuck Schaeffer, Vantive Media CEO

So, we ask you — as a CEO or C-suite executive — is your organization customer-centric?

How do you know? How can you tell? You may be able to answer that by asking yourself just one more question...

How often do you, your leaders and your employees share real customer experience stories in daily conversations?

Why is that the question to ask? Because, C-suite executives who are serious about customer-centricity are making the intentional decision to elevate and activate Voice of the Customer (VoC) in their companies and cultures. How are they doing this? Well, one thing they commit to is storytelling. That's right. From executive-level, decision-making discussions to day-to-day frontline employee conversations — real customer experience stories are omnipresent and shared on a consistent basis.

Think about your company and your culture. How often are real customer stories shared?

Are customer experience stories present in daily conversations across your business? Do they play a role in strategic and tactical decisions? Or are most of these conversations and decisions internally focused? Operational or product-driven? This simple gut check will tell you if you and your executive team are serious about Voice of the Customer. It will also help you understand if you are fully utilizing the power and influence real customer stories can have in your culture, your customer experience and on business performance.

Why do leading companies ensure real customer experience stories are omnipresent?

Because, what goes unmentioned ... is quickly forgotten. So, if you're not talking about the customer consistently — how can you really be a customer-centric organization? And the best way to elevate the Voice of the Customer is through real customer experience stories.

When most executives think of customer stories, they think of case studies. But case studies are not stories. They are simply a documented set of facts.

Stories are emotional. Stories bring real-world actions and outcomes to life. And most importantly, there is a moral (lesson learned) to every story. That's why customer stories play such a significant role in customer-centric cultures and companies.

The bottom-line impact of customer stories.

According to a recent *Harvard Business Review* article, "Research shows that end users (customers) ... who benefit from a company's products and services — are surprisingly effective in motivating employees to work harder, smarter and more productively." Another study showed that the simple act of sharing a story about how an employee impacted a customer's life can reinforce one's conviction about their purpose.

The fact is, when employees know their behaviors and actions matter and make a difference in the customer experience — they truly care. The article went on to say, "When employees share their stories about experiences with customers, they create a channel of mutual inspiration."

Simply put, elevating VoC through real customer experience stories impacts organizational performance, and ultimately, your bottom line.

As a C-suite executive, you can preach all day about the critical impact employee decisions and actions have on the customer, but often this goes in one ear and out the other. Executives can talk about how the company is making a difference in the world, but without real stories that illustrate the impact the company is having on customer lives ... the message falls flat.

What are you doing to elevate and activate real customer experience stories across your company?

If your answer is not much or nothing at all — that needs to change. Make this the year you leverage the power of customer stories to improve organizational clarity, alignment and performance.

About the Author

James O'Gara is a thought leader and serial entrepreneur in the field of communications. He is currently the CEO and Founder of OnMessage, a strategic B2B communications consultancy based in Dallas, Texas. He is also the founder of StoryDimensions, a SaaS sales enablement company that provides B2B customer stories and insights to sales teams ... at scale. In addition, he is the executive editor of CEO Communicator, the digital magazine for c-suite executives who aspire to achieve excellence in communications.

O'Gara has spent thousands of hours formulating winning go-to-market strategies and stories for dozens of Fortune 100 companies and hundreds of high-growth businesses. His expertise in go-to-market strategy development, customer research, messaging and positioning, as well as customer-centric culture development, has earned him the respect of executives around the world. His ability to breakdown strategy, sales, marketing and positioning challenges in complex industries has been invaluable to CEOs and CMOs at a number of leading companies.

To contact Mr. O'Gara, email him directly at: jogara@itsonmessage.com.

Made in the USA
Middletown, DE
30 September 2020